SUPERVISORY MANAGEMENT AND
ITS LINK TO THE HUMAN RESOURCES FUNCTION

SUPERVISORY MANAGEMENT AND ITS LINK TO THE HUMAN RESOURCES FUNCTION

Mohammed Salleh
and
Donald Grunewald

Mellen Studies in Business
Volume 6

The Edwin Mellen Press
Lewiston•Queenston•Lampeter

Library of Congress Cataloging-in-Publication Data

Salleh, Mohammed.
    Supervisory management and its link to the human resources function / Mohammed.
Salleh and Donald Grunewald.
        p. cm. -- (Mellen studies in business ; v. 6)
    Includes index.
    ISBN 0-7734-7484-6
    1. Supervision of employees. 2. Supervisors. 3. Personnel management. I. Grunewald,
Donald. II. Title. III. Series.

HF5549.12 .S236 2001
658.3'02--dc21

                                                                    00-065364

This is volume 6 in the continuing series
Mellen Studies in Business
Volume 6 ISBN 0-7734-7484-6
MSB Series ISBN 0-88946-152-X

A CIP catalog record for this book is available from the British Library.

The Edwin Mellen Press   The Edwin Mellen Press
        Box 450   Box 67
Lewiston, New York   Queenston, Ontario
USA 14092-0450   CANADA L0S 1L0

The Edwin Mellen Press, Ltd.
Lampeter, Ceredigion, Wales
UNITED KINGDOM SA48 8LT

Printed in the United States of America

DEDICATION

This book is dedicated to our wives, Kasara A. Kareem and Barbara S. Frees. We thank them for their encouragement and support and for their love.

TABLE OF CONTENTS

Preface 1

Acknowledgements 3

Abstract 5

Chapter 1:   The Supervisor 7

Chapter 2:   Administrative and Safety Management 21

Chapter 3:   Planning and Organization 33

Chapter 4:   Recruitment 47

Chapter 5:   Training and Development 59

Chapter 6:   Communication 69

Chapter 7:   Morale and Motivation 83

Chapter 8:   Counseling 97

Chapter 9:   Effective Supervisory Management 107

Chapter 10: Concluding Thoughts 119

General Index 129

TABLE OF ILLUSTRATIONS

FIGURE	TITLE	PAGE
1.0	Levels of Management	10
1.1	Supervisory Responsibilities	17
3.0	Budget for Test Operations	37
4.0	Recruitment and Selection Process	48
4.1	A Typical Advertisement	54
5.0	Learning Curve Chart	66
7.0	Objectives of Performance Appraisals	92
8.0	Functions of Counseling	99

PREFACE

by Dr. Edward C. Yang

Supervisory Management and its Link to the Human Resource Function *provides an excellent description of the role of the supervisor as a front line manager in a modern organization. The supervisor is the person in the middle between top management and workers. The modern organization depends upon the supervisor for its ultimate success.*

Supervisors deal directly with workers in helping them carry out the tasks required by the organization. To do this successfully, supervisors must perform many human relations functions that are often assumed to be performed by the human resources department of the company. To implement this, the supervisor must lead workers to success in accomplishing the goals of the organization. The supervisor must interface with both the workers and with top management. The supervisor must motivate and train the workers that are supervised. In addition, the supervisor must carry out the administrative tasks of the supervisory management position. The supervisor must also respond to the changing external environment with strategies and actions that will be effective.

This book provides a useful guide to the supervisor to achieve success in supervisory management. It also is useful to scholars and teachers in higher education who help prepare future managers for practical careers in management.

One of the great strengths of this book is that it includes practical examples of proficient supervisory management. Each of the authors of this book have both practical and academic experience in management.

Dr. Mohammed Salleh is currently the managing director of a well-known executive training organization in Singapore. He has written numerous scholarly articles on supervision and management. Dr. Salleh has extensive experience in management in supervisory positions and has served as a university faculty member teaching management. He is one of the Commonwealth's leading experts on training and supervision and a Fellow of the Royal Society of Arts.

Dr. Donald Grunewald has extensive experience as a faculty member and administrator in American universities and colleges. He served for twelve years as president of Mercy College in New York and is currently Professor of Strategic Management at the Hagan School of Business at Iona College. He has served as a consultant with corporations and with nonprofit and government organizations. He also has written extensively on management topics for academic and professional journals and is the author of twelve books including The Complete Book of Management *(co-authored with Dr. Sol Shaviro of Touro College), which was published by The Edwin Mellen Press in 1998. Dr. Grunewald is a Fellow of the Royal Society of Arts and of other scholarly organizations in the United States and in The United Kingdom.*

I recommend this book to anyone who wishes to know more about supervisory management and its link to the human resources function in a global economy.

Edward C. Yang, M.A. (Columbia University), M.S., Ph.D. (New York University). Former Professor of Economics and Business Administration at Fairleigh Dickinson University and City University of New York; President, John Dewey Foundation for International Education.

ACKNOWLEDGEMENTS

The authors would like to acknowledge the time, effort and useful advice given by a number of persons to help us complete this book. First of all, we would like to acknowledge the assistance of Dr. Christopher Clark who is the Senior Consultant for Drake Beam Morin Plc (U.K) and the Vice President of the Association of Cost & Executive Accountants (U.K.) for his assistance and advice.

We acknowledge the help of academic colleagues who have encouraged us to write this book. We especially acknowledge the support of the Dean of the Hagan School of Business at Iona College, Nicholas J. Beutell, Ph.D.

The authors are very grateful to Ms. Jilline Beh for her support with the initial draft of the manuscript. We thank Ms. Judie Szuets for her editorial help and for her producing the final two drafts of this book.

The support of the entire staff of our publisher, The Edwin Mellen Press, is gratefully acknowledged. In particular, we wish to acknowledge the helpful guidance and support of Dr. John Rupnow, the Director of The Edwin Mellen Press, and of Mrs. Patricia Schultz, the Production Manager of The Edwin Mellen Press.

We wish to acknowledge the help of Dr. Edward C. Yang, who has written the Preface for this book and who has helped with his suggestions and his review of this book for the publisher. We also thank Dr. Philip Baron, Visiting Professor of Florida Atlantic University for reviewing our book for the publisher and for his helpful advice.

4

The authors take full responsibility for any errors and omissions in this book. We are grateful to all those who helped us complete this book. We also appreciate the kindness of those who have decided to read this book. We hope that it will be useful to all those who read it.

ABSTRACT

The supervisor, being a front line manager, plays the pivotal role between largely abstract top management at one end and largely operational personnel at the other. How supervisors perform in this often frustrating but nevertheless crucial role is probably the biggest single factor in the success or failure of modern organizations.

*Recognizing the above, this study was undertaken to demonstrate the fact that, over and above the increasingly complex and difficult tasks that supervisory management staff have to deal with, they also have to act as **"mini personnel managers"** in their own right. The study focuses on the basic functions and related techniques as well as human relations for effective supervision. It also discusses the supervisor's role as leader, communicator, motivator, trainer and administrator. In the final chapter, it delineates the future perspectives of the changing environment facing supervisors and possible strategies for supervisory success.*

The goal of this study throughout has been to make the text easily understandable and applicable. As such, practical examples are quoted where possible. It is very much hoped that having grasped this blend of conceptual, functional and human relations insights and skills, the present or potential supervisor should be able to meet the challenges of supervision and the future as effectively as possible.

1
The Supervisor

Most people probably believe that they have a good idea of who supervisors are and what they actually do. For example, some may picture the supervisor as the person at a fast food establishment who runs frantically from one counter to another, shouting, "Faster! Faster!" Others may visualize a supervisor as the person in a manufacturing plant with arms folded and frowning at operators who tend to slow down from time to time. Another view of a supervisor reported is that of a person in authority who collects time cards, assigns the daily work orders, manages raw materials and schedules machines for maintenance.

However, despite the obvious differences and inaccuracies in these various depictions of supervisors and the supervision work they do, they all have at least two things in common:

a. Supervisors seldom or never actually perform the physical or manual nature of the work they oversee.

b. Supervisors are directly responsible for accomplishing the goals of their respective organizations through the management of the human and physical resources under their control.

These two significant aspects of the supervisor's job are sometimes difficult to resolve. They, in fact, pose a dilemma. On one hand, supervisors are responsible for the seamless work production in their areas of responsibilities; on the other hand, they are restricted from actually doing the work themselves. This unique situation has stimulated much attention over the years from researchers and writers on management theory and practice.

This study will delve into the various roles that supervisors play and show how their trained capabilities in management help the organization to achieve its goals. The following literature will explain how personnel management techniques are used by supervisors in their daily duties to carry out the work assigned to them. In particular, it will focus on the human relations approach to supervision, as well as administrative management.

1.1   The Supervisor and the Organization

One of the most difficult things to establish in any organization structure is the difference between the various grades of management, from the highest to the lowest ranks. It is important to note that the lower one goes in the hierarchy, the more particular and specialized the technical aspects of the supervisor's job become. The result is that there are often a very large number of different supervisory jobs even within one organization. For example, a production supervisor in factory **A** could control 15 operatives and a collection of testing equipment and personal computers that deal in digital and electronic scanning. However, another supervisor within the same organization but based in factory **B** could supervise 50 operatives and take care of a dozen manual work tools.

Bearing this in mind, any definition we assign must address this wide variety of jobs, responsibilities and status. Generally speaking, a reasonable part of the definition is that a supervisor is a member of the most junior level of management in the organization. Having noted this, focus shifts to the position that a supervisor occupies.

1.1.1   The Link Person

Countless definitions have been found in textbooks and journals alike that emphasize the supervisor being a link person between what is usually perceived as two opposing forces—management on one end, and the work force on the other. Supervising is often defined as *the overseeing of a process, its workers plus the linking of these employees with the top levels of management.* This is the unique challenge for supervisors as they cope with these two opposing forces. In order to do this effectively, the supervisor has to master the art of communicating with the workers in their language and the management in theirs.

Although supervisors are link persons in certain aspects of their jobs, they are, however, no more or no less than any other levels of management. This is because management itself has a series of levels; it can be argued that any level existing between two others has a link between the level above and that below. This is depicted in *Figure 1.0.* The fact very much remains that the functions of managers and supervisors are indistinguishable. It is the differences in emphasis that perhaps distinguish managers from supervisors.

1.1.2 Manager

Basically, the job of a manager normally comprises planning, organizing, controlling, communicating and motivating. One can see from these major functions that they are reasonably well suited to both managerial and supervisory jobs.

A possible definition of a managerial role is as follows:

> "It is any role in an organization where the occupant is authorized to get part of the work done through employed subordinates for whose work he or she remains accountable."

Such a definition however, is equally applicable to supervisors as it is to managers.

Other definitions stress differences between supervision and management in terms of the closeness of supervision. That is to say, supervisors operate at close range whereas management controls remotely. Such views contain an error of interpretation. This is because even when a manager controls direct operatives remotely, he or she has to give immediate focus to the staff he or she deals with, i.e., the supervisors.

It is therefore a fact that every manager is a supervisor and every supervisor is a manager. It is to be noted that in order to recognize this,

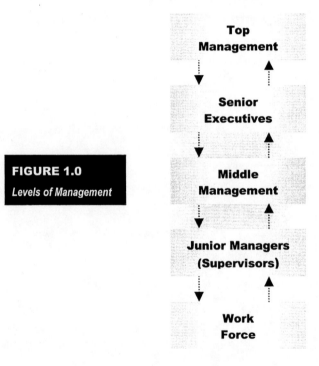

FIGURE 1.0

Levels of Management

Top Management

Senior Executives

Middle Management

Junior Managers (Supervisors)

Work Force

the supervisors' professional association in the United Kingdom has incorporated both words in its name—"The Institute of Supervisory

Management." However, there is a distinction between other managers and those of the first level that is quite clear and well defined.

The supervisor is part of the management team, but is distinct in the sense that the supervisor's subordinates are not managers, but operatives. The supervisor is a person given authority for planning and controlling the work of his or her group, but all he or she can delegate to the group is the work itself.

1.2 Front Line Manager

The supervisor is the official manager of the work group under his or her charge. Just like a manager, the supervisor is responsible for determining objectives, planning/organizing, communicating, controlling and motivating. Quite apart from all this, however, the basic roles of the supervisor as a first-line manager of his or her work group are:

a. Defining the roles for subordinates

b. Dealing with the problems of staff

c. Liaising with colleagues

d. Dealing with his or her immediate superior

e. Liaising with trade union representatives

As far as the workers are concerned, the supervisor is seen to represent management. On the other hand, however, management looks upon supervisory staff as the link to the workers. Yet, it is essential that the supervisor speaks and acts with the authority of his or her own position. Much of the success of the supervisor depends on how well this is done.

1.2.1 Defining the Work Roles of Subordinates

Each and every supervisor has the important role of defining subordinates' work roles in the workplace. It is an extremely difficult task to make jobs suit each individual. This is especially so at the operator level. By studying the nature of the job, selecting the methods to be used in performing the job and laying down the specifications and tolerances, the supervisor defines the work role of that job. Following this, the decision of whom to allocate the job to arises. In most cases at direct operative level, it is the individuals who have to be fitted to the jobs.

In defining the work role of a particular job, supervisors would normally follow set objectives that commit to projected outcomes of activity and are expressed as an expected result. As such, it should be very specific in nature, without any ambiguity. It must present a challenge and generate a thought-provoking process. Further to this, it must be measurable and fixed targets need to be set against which operators judge their performance. Above all, the standards that have been set must be achievable—a poor set of standards might cause morale problems.

1.2.2 Dealing with Staff Problems

This is one of the most difficult aspects of supervisory management. A supervisor has to handle the workers' moods and difficult attitudes amidst work pressure. The supervisor needs to secure workers' co-operation and motivate them, resolve individual problems and counsel them whenever a situation calls for it. Skillful management techniques and a good understanding of human nature is required with an appreciation for the fact that a little praise goes a long way.

In handling complaints and grievances, it is prudent to understand what a grievance is. A *grievance* is any situation or act that is unfair in the mind of the complainer. If a worker imagines that he has a problem, then he has a grievance. Once a supervisor suspects that a particular staff member has a problem (grievance), the supervisor acts quickly, as most fires can be put out with a cup of water if applied at the right time and place. Swift reaction is important because if the small problems are taken care of, the larger ones may never develop.

Basically, front line managers need to distinguish between on-job and off-job causes to problems. Regarding on-job causes, it is usually the case that most grievances arise from a lack of understanding of the purpose behind various regulations and orders issued by management. Other causes may lie within the areas of control and communication. Additional causes can include favoritism in assigning work, credit stealing and the lack of supervisory interest in the work or the workers themselves. The following are the probable off-job causes:

a. housing difficulties

b. domestic troubles

c. financial problems, and

e. personal disturbances

Supervisors would normally have to act to fix a problem once it is deemed to be interfering in any way with work output or performance. Advising workers to "forget it" will *never* achieve a satisfactory result.

1.2.3 Liaising with Colleagues

Other supervisory colleagues and supervisory group staff would come to expect a supervisor to cooperate and maintain relevant standards that have been set in the workplace. They look toward the supervisor to complete his or her part of the total task well and on time.

Here, compromise and conciliation are the order of the day. A supervisor cannot in any way enforce requirements, but rather must persuade and justify his or her requests, which is not a bad exercise in itself. Good communication skills are obviously vital as they can be used to gain rapport and trust with counterparts.

1.2.4 Own Immediate Supervisor

Dealing with one's own immediate supervisor is no easy task. The superior may be domineering, weak, unapproachable, distant and difficult to talk to, or good at the job and able to lead well, competent, or somewhere in between. The supervisor has to receive instructions and orders and pass them on, and see whether they are carried out through effective follow-up. In return, the supervisor has to provide line feedback and advise on likely events that may occur. The supervisor needs to relay this information either verbally or in written report form to his or her supervisors.

A supervisor is expected to envision what it is like to be in the manager's role and try to imagine the problems and difficulties facing the manager. This means that the supervisor will make a better guide and assistant if he or she is able to see others' point of view as well as his or her own. To put it in a nutshell, the supervisor as a boss in one sphere—with his or her work group—and subordinate in another—the staff of the boss—will find all his or her actions viewed from two perspectives. This makes it quite impossible for the supervisor to please everyone at any given time.

1.2.5 Industrial Relations

In basic terms, industrial relations usually denotes the relationships between employer and employees in all work situations. What this means to the supervisor is that as a representative of management, his or her dealings with workers in every situation must be perceived as just and fair. The local union representative has the very same responsibility.

Samuel Gompers, a prominent United States union official, once said, "The greatest disservice a company can do to workers is to run an unprofitable operation." In this respect, both the supervisor and the union representative should have a real concern for the economic viability of the organization at heart. To this end, the supervisor has an important role to play. As far as it is appropriate, the supervisor should:

a. Pass factual information at all times. This will kill rumors and beat the grapevine.

b. Consult on such things as pending changes.

c. Be well briefed on all the conditions of employment relating to the work group and the legal requirements that concern his or her activities.

d. Ensure that he or she is the first contact regarding complaints and grievances.

e. Know clearly how to handle disciplinary matters.

The union representative speaks on behalf of the members and has position to influence. The supervisor, on the other hand, has an assigned responsibility and authority. However, even so, the supervisor is, to a degree, dependent upon his or her influence with the group. Perhaps the most significant point that management must recognize is that the supervisor must be kept clearly and fully informed at all times.

Although it may seem that the supervisor is expected to control several roles, the supervisor need not in actual fact do all these things simultaneously. The supervisor's strength lies in the ability to manage priorities. There will definitely be conflicting demands on the supervisor's time but conscious choices of priorities must be made. There are four major responsibilities and within each there can exist conflicting needs. The primary task of the supervisor is to get work done that will achieve objectives. With this in mind, the supervisor then assesses other priorities according to the circumstances of the situation and the effects of their impact.

1.3   Trained Capabilities of Supervisors

A well rounded supervisor is required to have in-depth technical knowledge, well developed management skills, orientation control, the right attitude and a sense of urgency to carry out the task even with difficult setbacks. These are essential qualities that make for supervisory success.

Technical Competence. The qualifications necessary for the supervisor's job are impressive. Supervisors need to be technically competent; that is, knowing the product and its specifications, the machinery and its capabilities, the processes employed and the reasons why these processes are necessary and relevant. Further to this, technical competence means knowing the organization's rules or provisions of collective bargaining agreements, if they exist. It means knowing the labor laws and other government regulations that apply to the business. It must be noted, however, that this knowledge cannot be superficial—vague ideas about product specifications or schedule requirements could very well jeopardize management's plans. Supervisors need in-depth knowledge, as they are the resource people for the workers. This can only be accomplished by developing a thorough technical competency.

Good People Skills. Employees are selected to be supervisors because, among other things, they are good workers. Most often, new supervisors fail

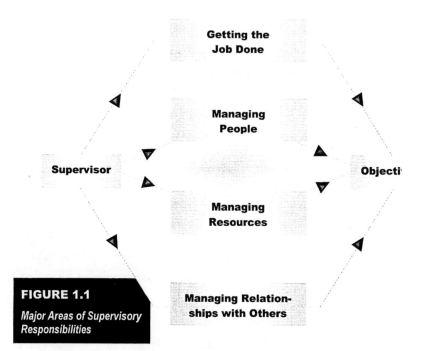

Getting the Job Done

Managing People

Supervisor

Objecti

Managing Resources

FIGURE 1.1

Major Areas of Supervisory Responsibilities

Managing Relationships with Others

not because they lack technical know-how, but rather because they are unable to get others to work effectively for them. In other words, *they lack human management skills.* It is necessary to make mental adjustments. The performance traits that qualify one for promotion, for example, have to do with one's individual effectiveness. As a hands-on, new employee, the supervisor was productive at his job. He or she had the right attitude. This is where a transition becomes necessary. The supervisor's individual effort, productivity and attitude become less important to success as he or she is promoted to supervisory ranks. Instead, the supervisor must now get the group to do what management wants them to and what the supervisor was able to do so well as a worker. It could be an advantage if the supervisor can instill enthusiasm and commitment in the people that he or she supervises. In other words, he must have leadership qualities. In many countries today, such as Singapore and the United States, working with people means working with people of various cultures and ethnic groups. This poses an additional problem for the supervisor. The supervisor may have to be fluent in at least two languages, as some operators may not understand the English language. The supervisors have to communicate using clear, concise language in order to be understood by all workers. Cultural differences must also be recognized and dealt with carefully. The important thing is that supervisors must understand that each individual be treated fairly so as to be able to gain their respect, patience and understanding.

Sense of Urgency. All supervisors should have a well-developed "sense of urgency." This is, in fact, often a precarious balance between panic and apathy. The supervisor sets the tone for the work group, and a necessary ingredient is that all the day's primary objectives must be met. Not only are they to be met, they must be met in the way in which the supervisor directs. The supervisor conveys the view that assignments are necessary, schedules are commitments and budgets are legitimate and to be followed. If assignments are to be carried out on the basis of convenience, the supervisor and the department are wasting precious time. It is tempting to schedule service work or optional tasks based on our own convenience. However, this assumes that there will be no "inconveniences," such as rush orders, power failures or employee illnesses. This is imperative for supervisors to understand and they should strive to approach every daily assignment as though each piece of work requires immediate attention. In such a way, the chances of getting caught short are greatly reduced.

Controls. Company controls, such as budgets, schedules, performance standards and so on, are all necessary to keep people on the right track and to achieve the desired results. Effective supervisors develop departmental controls that do for them what the larger controls do for the company's management—that is, channeling everyone's efforts in the desired direction to help reach the collective goals. Many of these departmental controls will be the same as the overall company controls because the supervisor's responsibility is to meet, on a reduced scale, these larger company objectives. Other controls instituted may be personal. For example, supervisors may want certain queries directed to them rather than others. If employees need equipment repaired, supervisors may set procedures for relevant forms to be signed off by them instead of having line operators highlight the problem directly to the maintenance section. Also, supervisors must appreciate that when controls are put in place, they have the effect of focusing attention on these areas. If supervisors constantly monitor these control points, employees are not likely to stray from the desired path.

Right Attitude. Finally, an extremely important point for achieving success is the personal quality of having the right attitude towards one's employees. In a very real sense, the expectations of the company and the supervisor go a long way towards shaping the attitudes and performance of the employees. It has been found that when supervisors convey to the workers high expectations for their performance, those workers try to perform up to the level of that expectation. When little is expected of them, the workers behave accordingly. The trick to this is to help people reach their potential. This can be done by giving them job training, setting high performance targets within reasonable standards, as well as by setting an example, showing that they can accomplish difficult but achievable tasks with strong mindsets and diligent work efforts.

2

Administrative and Safety Management

PART I. ADMINISTRATION

Generally speaking, administration has a very wide scope in management. Just as there is industrial administration in the field of business management, supervisory management has certain fundamental requirements in basic administration. This chapter looks into the general administrative duties of supervisors, the office equipment they use and the project reports they write.

2.1 Administrative Duties

When supervisors are recruited into an organization, they are usually briefed on the administrative duties that must be addressed on the shop floor. This is typically done during an induction session. Certain administration is meant to cater to higher management's requirements while others are meant for the personnel or human resources department and payroll purposes.

In an electronics manufacturing plant, for example, the following are some of the common administrative duties that a supervisor has to attend to:

a. Daily attendance tracking

b. Annual leave forecasting

c. Time/pay cards verification

d. Updating of performance records

e. Weekly/monthly status reports

f. Labor measurement reports

Duties **a** through **c**, if administered accurately, would help the personnel or human resources department in monitoring staff presence, as well as in advising the finance department regarding offsetting any annual or medical leave entitlement in the company records. Duty four—keeping an up-to-date individual staff performance record—aids the supervisor in assessing subordinates when it comes time for performance appraisals. It is an important piece of data that reflects staff efficiency and effectiveness.

The last two indicated duties, whereby reports are generated, are meant to cater to management's needs. The status and labor measurement reports show top management the activities carried out in the area under the supervisor's coverage and the standards that are being achieved. It is, in fact, an assessment of the supervisor's performance. In addition to this, as a coordinator in the work area, the supervisor generates memoranda whenever necessary to various departments and sections to enlist support and help, or to highlight potential problems to management. In certain organizations, supervisors holding staff meetings also have to ensure that minutes are recorded and published for circulation to all relevant parties concerned.

2.2 Office Equipment Used

The provision and the use of office machinery combines labor and capital in the pursuit of greater efficiency. There are several advantages to be gained in using office equipment. The use of them saves time and this is an important advantage when an assignment has to be completed by a deadline. They promote accuracy and relieve the drudgery of conventional handwritten methods. They enhance the appearance of output, especially reports and letters, and lessen the fatigue of the staff, thereby improving the quality of output.

Listed below are some of the office equipment that supervisors use in their day-to-day work activities:

a. Personal computers

b. Photocopying machines

c. Adding/calculation machines

Personal computers (which include the use of spreadsheet programs, such as Lotus or Excel; word processing applications, such as Word or WordPerfect; page layout software, such as PageMaker or Quark; and so on) are probably the most widely used equipment in recent years. The truly remarkable word processing technique followed the invention of the automatic electric typewriter. The major advantages of personal computers are the speed of word processing and the ability to store large volumes of data. Retrieval of information stored in its memory is instantaneous. The storage of data on personal computers is by floppy diskettes or hard disk drives. Printing out work completed is also very easy. Once a printer is connected to the computer, all one needs to do to print is retrieve the stored data. Upon activation of a print command, a perfectly printed document will be produced. Another advantage is the elimination of paper drafts for editing as revisions can be entered directly to the file, which is displayed on a full-screen monitor. The full-screen display also facilitates easier formatting of documentation. Calculations can also be easily accomplished on the personal computer when the user enters addition, subtraction, division or multiplication formulas.

Photocopying is a method of copying a page with photographic detail and is generally used to obtain one or more copies of documents. The photocopy machine is very widely used and is now a necessity in most offices. The advantages are that exact facsimile copies are obtained of every detail. When few copies are required, as is usually so, it is often the cheapest form of duplicating. Sophisticated features of copiers today include reduction or enlargement of image capabilities, double-sided copying, collation of several copies and even stapling. Finally, it is also a very fast means of duplicating. Use of e-mail and the Internet permits files to be circulated widely and directly from a workstation—this is advantageous to today's worker from both a time and cost standpoint.

The electronic and electronic programmable calculators are the most commonly used form of calculators. The characteristics of these calculators include figures that are shown in lighted electronic displays. Calculations are performed electronically. These calculators are fully automatic and function at great speed. For programmable calculators, they are halfway to being a computer, insofar as they perform calculations automatically in accordance with a standard program. Both these electronic calculators are quiet in operation.

2.3 Project Reports

A supervisor in the course of work in a manufacturing sector is often called upon to undertake a project either to solve certain existing problems or to improve aspects of the work process. A project is basically an investigation of a problem or situation with the objective of collecting relevant and appropriate information, analyzing it, then arriving at logical conclusions and making recommendations. After completing a project, supervisors present it in report form. A report is a written document setting out what has been discovered after investigation, plus comments, opinions, evaluations and recommendations. At the same time it gives information, reports findings and draws conclusions.

The different types of projects that supervisors usually tackle can generally be divided into three categories:

a. Problem solving

b. Descriptive

c. Cost saving

Problem Solving. These can be situations such as the ever-increasing costs and inconveniences associated with repairing and maintaining aging equipment and machinery. The resolution of such projects will result from an analysis of the effects on a particular section and the organization it served (if no change was made) set against the cost and inconvenience of replacing the equipment with new and expensive, but more flexible equipment. Another example is the problem of what to do with underutilized repair capacity, errors arising out of inadequate procedures and so on. By far, the largest number of projects come under this heading.

Descriptive (Procedure) Reports. Sometimes supervisors come across a different kind of problem—that of setting out procedures for the first time. This could come about when there are no established procedures and the existing method of training is one of getting an employee familiarized by observing an experienced staff. In this case, a clear and detailed procedural manual could be drawn up.

Cost Saving. In a sense, "problem solving" projects could, as a byproduct, save costs, but there are some projects that set out to save money right from the start. An example of such a project was one in which a 28 port Winchester disk drive electronic testing equipment was converted into a 56 port machine by connecting additional power relays and connectors, thus reorienting the position of the disk drives being tested. This project doubled the testing capacity and a considerable amount of funds were saved in not requiring the purchase of new testing equipment.

In all the above-mentioned types of reports, there are certain requirements and sequences of events that need to be taken into account before a project can be started. Supervisors undertaking projects usually set out both a checklist and a timetable prior to embarking on a project. The following is a brief sample outline of a project checklist and timetable.

PROJECT CHECKLIST

❐ Identification of problem

❐ Terms of reference

❐ Plan to obtain basic information

❐ Title of report summarized

❐ Glossary for technical language

❐ Types of graphs, charts and diagrams required

❐ Suitable layout for the project

❐ Clarity of the report

PROJECT TIMETABLE	BY
❐ Discuss the project with supervisors	Mid January
❐ Finalize terms of reference—decide on methods of investigation	February
❐ Carry out investigations	June completio
❐ First draft work and layout	Early July
❐ Finalize second draft work with supervisor	Early August
❐ Completed report for submission	End August

One of the most important things that supervisors writing project reports always bear in mind is that the report is meant for a reader, in this case a superior. As such, the more clearly and precisely the data is presented, the sooner the points made will get home.

PART II. SAFETY

One of the major contributions to health and safety by H.W. Heinrich, a safety engineer who studied accidents on American railways in the 1920s, was to place responsibility firmly upon people. Unexplained accidents or "acts of God" sometimes did occur, but in Heinrich's experience accidents were typically caused by negligence. People at every level were responsible—management for inadequate focus on safety and failure at times to educate and train the labor force properly, and the work people for their lack of awareness about the need to care. Recognizing this, government authorities in many countries have introduced laws to ensure that occupational health and safety management is given the weighty consideration it deserves.

2.4   Safety: A Legal Obligation

Human suffering and added costs are not the only reasons management is concerned about workplace safety. Statutory laws, such as the *Factories Act* in Singapore or the regulations of the Occupational Safety and Health Administration (OSHA), require complete compliance regarding rules and regulations on occupational health and safety. Stiff penalties are meted out to those who are charged and convicted for violations of this law. As such, companies have a legal obligation to see that employees work in an environment that is free of hazards.

A common statutory law in many countries is the workman's compensation statute. This set of laws has several common features, including those listed here:

a. The laws provide for some repayment of lost income, payment of medical expenses, vocational rehabilitation, if necessary, and death benefits to survivors.

b. The workers do not have to sue to collect these benefits.

c. It is basically an insurance program with the premiums paid for by the employer.

d. An element of coinsurance exists because the worker's loss is not fully covered.

e. Medical expenses, however, are fully covered.

f. It is a no-fault system. All job-related injuries and illnesses are covered, regardless of who was responsible.

Workman's compensation laws were passed because they served the needs of both employers and workers. The employer accepted the liability for the costs of work-related injuries and diseases. Maximum payment limits were set. These limits were considerably less than the awards that might be earned in a lawsuit, which spared the employer the expensive payout that might be possible otherwise. However, for giving up the chance at receiving higher settlements, employees got prompt and certain payment. Thus, this arrangement gave both parties desired security—reasonable financial limits for employers and certainty of payment for eligible employees. Although the workman's compensation law does have its drawbacks, in recent years it has become an important employee benefit.

2.5 The Supervisor and Safety

In many countries, legal obligations exist for both supervisors and managers. These obligations can impact the supervisor in two ways—as agents for the employer or as employees themselves. However, in addition to the strictly legal role, the supervisor has the task of promoting and maintaining a high level of safety consciousness among the work force. Safety is not now nor has it ever been a particularly exciting topic. Indeed, it is often greeted with indifference or even open hostility, particularly where safety practices may be time-consuming, inconvenient and/or expensive.

The safety minded supervisor will not only do what is required by law and government regulations, but also try to involve the work force with his or her direct action or in collaboration with other supervisors. Whenever appropriate, the supervisor would also encourage staff to participate in company-wide programs that are devised by the personnel or human resources department. Listed below are some of the possible ways to improve safety consciousness among employees:

a. Role-playing simulated accidents with workers observing and trying to establish the causes and possible ways of prevention.

b. Competitions: These might vary from each employee being asked to find as many safety faults in the working environment as he or she can to running a suggestion plan to produce ideas for safer ways of working or organizing poster competitions with prizes for employees finding the greatest number of hazards.

c. Departmental safety committees, or even the involvement of every worker in safety discussions at regular intervals.

d. Running a selection of safety films or videocassettes for employee awareness.

e. Visits from inspectors, fire departments, ambulance personnel and others to advise and instruct employees in safety methods, the proper use of appliances and elementary first aid.

Organizations are also required to prepare and circulate safety policies as they apply to the whole organization. In order to create additional employee awareness, supervisors could create a similar working document, which would be applicable to their respective sections. There are also safety manuals for supervisors to read and select appropriate entices to be listed in a safety audit document. (For example, are all walkways, gangways and paths clearly marked?) Supervisors might also arrange for all employees to be involved in regular safety checks, with perhaps some recognition for those not only pointing out inadequacies or hazards but also offering viable solutions.

Finally, it has to be noted that a supervisor's example on the shop floor is important. In one instance cited, a safety officer stated that he often visited premises where management complained that employees would not observe the safety principle of wearing eye-shields in their work area. In this particular case, the manager of the particular department being inspected took the safety officer onto the shop floor to prove his statement, failing himself to wear an eye-shield. As the safety officer commented, how can workers be expected to be safety conscious when their superiors are not? This is an important factor that supervisors need to recognize.

2.6 Safety In the Workplace

One of the most important and continuing responsibilities of *all* employees is safety in the workplace. An accident is an unplanned event caused by an unsafe act or condition. Thus, the vital task for supervisors is to recognize these hazards and to take action to remedy them as quickly as possible. This will require:

a. Leadership and sharing responsibility

b. Compliance with all relevant laws and regulations

c. Maintenance of safe working conditions

d. Safety training and emergency drill

Job safety makes sense for a number of reasons. Pain and suffering can be reduced or avoided altogether. Injured workers often suffer loss of income.

Accidents raise the costs of doing business. Finally, there are the legal obligations on employers as delineated earlier in this chapter. They must see to it that the workplace is reasonably free of recognized hazards.

Even with these incentives, workplace accidents continue to be a major problem for most companies. Unfortunately, these employers see accidents occurring because of careless employees as well as unavoidable circumstances. Employees, on the other hand, believe that they are somehow personally immune from injuries. Strange as it may seem, they believe that accidents happen, but they happen only to other people. Employers and employees who have these views are obviously very mistaken. They share the blame for these hazards and accidents. Even worse, most workplace injuries could be easily prevented. Companies that follow a few simple procedures experience significant reductions in accident occurrences. Employees who observe the common sense safety rules seldom get hurt on the job.

Some safety problems are complex. They are beyond simple solution so they are best left to the safety and health professionals. Hazardous substances and the introduction of new technologies into the workplace are such examples. However, this does not mean that supervisors should not be aware of their responsibilities and see to it that a safe working environment exists for all employees.

Stress is yet another factor that impacts health and performance in the workplace. However, it is only recently that the effects of excessive stress on people has been recognized. But, as with accidents, most causes of stress can be dealt with if supervisors are aware of the sources and symptoms. For that matter, supervisors also face stress themselves. They must, therefore, develop coping techniques if they are to be fully effective on the job.

One important fact that management needs to take note of is that workplace injuries tend to rise during periods of improved business. Overtime is worked, machines are operated for longer intervals and maintenance of equipment and machinery are postponed for slower periods. New employees are hired in large intakes as manpower requirement increases. Current employees get assigned to unfamiliar jobs and supervisors find that they are spread thinner than usual while taking on additional duties. These conditions add substantially to the risks in the workplace. Thus, extra care needs to be taken during peak workload time periods.

3

Planning and Organization

The main objective of this chapter is to give a firm understanding and appreciation of the need for long-range planning. The relevant techniques and skills for utilizing and interpreting long-range planning methods such as budgeting, manpower planning, production planning/control and capacity will be discussed.

3.1 The Planning Process

Planning is a basic supervisory function. It is a process whereby a future state is desired and compared with the present one and specific steps are formulated and selected to achieve the future state. Although several combinations of possible actions may achieve stated goals, there are also some combinations that will not work. Effective planning would involve evaluating each possible action carefully with a view toward its impact on all other factors. Once a workable set of action plans has been determined, the planner must follow through. The plans must be communicated to the employees and resources allocated to make the necessary changes. The plans must be continually reassessed and modified to make sure that the projected goals are in fact being achieved.

The following example could be used for a manufacturing supervisor. At the beginning of the week, the supervisor receives a production schedule indicating that the section must produce 600 units of product **X**, 450 units of product **Y** and 350 units of product **Z** by the end of the week. The supervisor then figures out the combination of manpower, machines, materials and money (cost) that would be necessary to achieve this goal.

These factors are known as the **4Ms** in planning. After considering a number of alternatives, the supervisor finally arrives at a plan that specifies the workers who will be assigned to particular tasks, and the machines and materials needed. If all goes well, the production goals for the week will be achieved.

Inherent in the definition of planning and the above example are the following aspects of the planning process.

a. **Goal Setting.** People need something to aim for. Countless studies have clearly demonstrated that when goals are challenging and realistic, people are motivated to achieve them.

b. **Setting Measurements and Standards.** Plans, goals and activities should always be stated in terms that can be observable and measurable. This is because the standard of measurement serves both a control and feedback function. Both supervisors and employees are able to evaluate their progress when objective standards have been clearly specified.

c. **Maintaining a Time Perspective.** All plans are designed to provide guidance through some defined time period. Once time periods are specified, they serve as objective timeframes for the planner and participants.

d. **Specifying Alternatives.** As shown in the example earlier, there is a wide range and many combinations of variables that may affect the achievement of a goal. Bearing this in mind, supervisors must be creative, open-minded and willing to consider all options.

e. **Analyzing Alternatives.** This is another critical stage in the planning process. Here all the variables and alternatives that have been defined are carefully weighed to determine some combination that will lead to the achievement of the desired goal.

f. **Ensuring Participation.** Carrying out the plan requires the support and participation of the workers of the organization. Several methods and philosophies of planning, such as MBO (management by objectives), emphasize the need for participation throughout the planning process. There is ample research to demonstrate that both the quality of the plans attained and the motivation to achieve these plans increase when employees participate in the planning process.

g. **Maintaining Communication.** Only when organizational goals and the plans to achieve them are effectively communicated to those involved can they be achieved.

h. **Organizing.** The main idea behind any planning process is the organization of the activities into an integrated and unified pattern that guides everyone toward the desired objectives.

i. **Implementing.** Plans are useless unless they are followed. Plans must have complete and total support from top management, supervisors and the workers carrying it out. For implementation to be successful, plans must be viewed as an integral part of everyone's job.

j. **Follow-up.** Every plan must have provisions for periodic review. As plans become more specific, measurable guideposts for achievements should be indicated so that individuals know where they are in relation to achieving the overall objectives.

k. **Flexibility.** Plans are never fixed. They must be viewed as dynamic and ever changing. Various circumstances may warrant a change. Thus, planning is not a process with a defined beginning and end but a continuing process.

I. **Planning for Contingencies.** Because planning hinges on the future, it is subject to all the hazards of any type of forecasting procedure. Factors such as lack of sufficient information, changes in supply and demand of personnel, raw materials and lack of time perspective are some examples. However, even though these factors may affect supervisory plans, their impact is much more critical when no attempt is made to assess them. The planning process helps supervisors to anticipate and account for these variables rather than react to them helplessly.

All of the aspects listed here are extremely important for developing a realistic and concrete conceptual framework for the planning process.

3.2 Budget Forecast

Budgets are among the most important and common planning devices for most organizations. Very simply, budgets are the expression in quantitative terms of plans for the future.

Although a budget may be presented in one lump sum, supervisors are most frequently required to itemize specific expenditures so that the spending can be better controlled. The actual format for the budget differs in almost every organization. *Figure 3.0* shows a typical budget.

The budget serves two major functions. First, it allows the management of the organization to evaluate and assess the efficiency and contributions of each unit in the organization. Second, and more important from the perspective of planning, budgets provide a pooled estimate of the organization's capital needs over a period of time. Accordingly, the financial people in the organization can manage money to ensure that it will be available when needed. When budgets are overestimated, it can be extremely costly for the organization. Just as individuals must pay interest to finance automobiles and homes, so must organizations finance their needs through stocks, bonds, loans and mortgages.

FIGURE 3.0
Budget for Test Operations in Asian Factory

Items	Quantity	Unit Cost	Total Project Cost
Raw Materials			
Screws	50,000 pieces	$40.00 (per K)	$2,000.00
Washers	50,000 pieces	$45.00 (per K)	$2,250.00
PCBA (plastic circuit board assembly)	500 pieces	$60.00 (each)	$30,000.00
No. 5 Wire	20,000 ft.	$0.80 (per ft.)	$1,600.00
		Subtotal	$35,850.00
Maintenance			
Preventive Maintenance	20 hours	$12.00 (per hour)	$240.00
Downtime Maintenance	50 hours	$12.00 (per hour)	$600.00
		Subtotal	$840.00
Wages and Salary			
Supervisors	6 staff	$1,500.00	$9,000.00
Indirect Labor	12 staff	$750.00	$9,000.00
Direct Labor	180 staff	$500.00	$90,000.00
		Subtotal	$108,000.00
Miscellaneous			
Office Supplies	—	—	$5,000.00
		Grand Total	$149,690.00

The variety of plans made by an organization is reflected in the range of budgets that are in use. These budgets fall into two main types—capital and expense—that supervisors are most often called upon to produce.

a. *Capital budgets* are estimates of expenditures on items like new equipment. These would be regarded as an asset of the organization rather than as an expense.

b. *Expense budgets* cover the material and labor needed to achieve the forecast production or sales activities of a department. These are the everyday operating costs of the organization, and at a company level may include other overhead items, like interest on loans.

Some organizations set a minimum figure on items of expenditure to be included in capital estimates, but this is often a question of administrative convenience rather than logic. Thus, supervisors trained in department budgeting have to take into account such situations in their preparation of budgets. As capital expenditures and expense budgets are often treated differently by the tax authorities in many countries, it is important that expenses should be correctly located, otherwise unnecessary costs are incurred.

In addition to those already mentioned here, there are also cash budgets. The organization must have the cash resources to meet its commitments as they fall due. Income and expenditures are not constant over the year, and highlighting discrepancies should help to smooth out the occasions when there is either a cash surplus or a deficiency of cash. Although supervisors play only a small role in cash budgets, the monitoring of cash expenses and giving feedback on inappropriate spending plays a vital role in shaping cash budgets. There is little point in formally estimating costs for operational activities if the organization then runs out of cash funds for financing these activities. A cash budget emphasizes that departments create the need for cash, as well as bring in cash, through their activities.

Accurate budgets become critical to the health and survival of organizations, and significant pressure is placed on supervisors or managers who exceed or overestimate their budget. These pressures, in turn, have incented many creative but ultimately disadvantageous games that are often played with budgets. For example, sometimes budgets can be cut, say, ten percent for no apparent reason. The affected supervisor learns this game quickly and subsequently overestimates his next budget by at least ten percent. This forces top management to redefine its rules and regulations and escalate cuts to, say, twenty percent. This is a situation that needs to be avoided or eventually the overall organization becomes the big loser.

Another potential problem with budgets is that supervisors' salaries are sometimes tied to the size of their budgets. Thus, supervisors learn to strive for budget increases (which is not healthy) and see no incentives to budget or cost reduction programs. Some organizations, however, have become cognizant of this and provide substantial rewards and recognition for budget and cost reductions. Supervisors must attempt to cope with these potential problems with budgets because, regardless of some of the seemingly inventive ploys attempted, the budget will have a significant impact on their planning effectiveness and the organization's future fiscal health.

3.3   Production Planning and Control

The twin functions of the planning and control of production are closely related, and are primarily the responsibility of the section called the production planning group. However, supervisors are responsible for the control of production schedules and planning within the manufacturing section and frequently liaise closely with the planning group in this respect. They invariably hold the key to the success of plans through their execution of the pre-planned operational directives.

What is called the pre-planning stage usually covers matters relating to the products to be produced, the designs of those products and the size of outputs to be aimed for. In the case of an established organization, the question of what products to produce could refer to the type of model for specific products, such as a Winchester disk drive, that need to be manufactured. Thereafter, planning is required to ensure the most effective and economical coordination of materials, labor and machines. This effectively translates to the right places in the right quantities at the right times.

Control is defined as a function that checks to ensure that what was planned to happen does actually happen. Production control therefore requires that standards be set and targets established, and that actual performances be compared with these targets on a regular basis. Should performance deviate from the established and approved plans or standards, it is the function of production control to take the necessary corrective action without delay.

To put it simply, it can be said that the responsibility of the production planning and control function is to ensure smooth and uninterrupted production with the avoidance of holdups and bottlenecks. To achieve this, the following are necessary:

a. Close cooperation with purchasing, vendors and sales departments to ensure that materials are available when needed and that production keeps pace with sales. Production of various product models may have to be accelerated or slowed in accordance with the sizes of orders received and sales made.

b. Decisions on the methods of production to be employed, and the most effective sequence in which products will be produced. In some cases, priority may have to be given to the filling of specific orders.

c. Labor and machinery must be allocated in the most effective and economical way to meet targeted objectives.

d. Time schedules must be established for the various stages of the production processes.

e. Continuous methods of inspection must be established, together with methods for the control of costs incurred.

A production plan will be incorporated into a production program that will lay down the process involved, the sequence of operations, the time schedules for the completion of each operation and the final completion, the *"machine loadings"*—that is, the work allocated to each machine and work group. The program will have to be coordinated with the purchasing and vendor resources departments by the supervisor to ensure that the correct materials in the necessary quantities are available when required for each operation.

Progress control is necessary to ensure that production performances conform to the time schedules. It involves a continuous check on production outputs, determining the reasons for any deviation from the time schedules, resolving the problem or removing the cause of it, adjusting materials delivery if necessary and advising the sales department of any changes in planned delivery times or dates. The planning group, in liaison with the production supervisor, carries out the last stated action item. During this phase, the supervisor must provide feedback to the sales department immediately of any problems faced on the production floor so that the planning group, who does the expediting, is kept well aware of the situation at hand. Production schedules can be upset by the shortage of materials or labor, machinery breakdowns or power failures, technical errors, accidents and similar causes.

Inspection is essential to ensure that finished products reach the standards set forth. In recent times, manufacturing has introduced the *Total Quality Management [TQM]* concept, whereby manufacturing quality assurance is adopted on the shop floor. This plan makes workers responsible for their own work and encourages them to take pride in their quality work. It advocates the principle that quality cannot be inspected, but rather that it is built in. Any quality issues, like faulty electronic components or poor workmanship, need to be identified by the supervisor and remedial action taken where necessary. In cases where tolerances are permitted in standards that have been set, they must be clearly defined and accepted as a requirement. Another important function of inspection is to provide management with information about costs of deviation from specifications and missed delivery schedules, otherwise known as the price of non-conformance.

Work study is concerned with examining all aspects of production work, and is carried out with the objective of improving efficiency and reducing wasted effort—both of which will result in improved productivity. There are two areas of work study. The first is called *Motion Study* and its aim is to find ways of reducing time-wasting movement, such as locating tools or materials more conveniently for a machine operator. The second area is called *Work Measurement* and is concerned with measuring the time taken to perform the various activities involved in a task and, by adding up the various times, arriving at the total time taken to perform the entire task. Work measurement seeks to determine how long a certain job should take a qualified and experienced worker to perform, and the results can be used in setting performance standards.

For the line supervisors, it is necessary to observe closely any new methods or procedures in actual practice, investigate any variations from what was originally planned, and make any modifications found to be necessary in light of their experience.

3.4 Production Capacity

Determining the size of a facility is critical to an organization's success. In order to ensure that production targets set in accordance with sales requirements can be achieved, management needs to plan ahead to forecast its manufacturing capability. Supervisors play an important role in calculating capacity and providing feedback to management from the production floor level. In gathering feedback from the various manufacturing sections (i.e., from product assembly right up to the final packaging area), management uses this information to assess the overall plans in capacity planning.

In basic terms, capacity is the maximum output of a system in a given period. Capacity is normally expressed as a rate, such as the number of tons of steel that can be produced per week or the number of disk drives in terms of thousands that can be produced per month or per quarter. For many companies, measuring capacity can be straightforward. It is the maximum number of units that can be produced in a specific time.

However, for some organizations, determining capacity can be more unique. Capacity can be measured in terms of beds (a hospital), active members (a professional club), or the number of counselors (an educational institute). Other organizations use total time available as a measure of overall capacity.

The designed capacity of a facility is the maximum capacity that can be achieved under ideal conditions. Most organizations operate their facilities at a rate less than the designed capacity. They do so because they have found that they can operate more efficiently when their resources are not stretched to the limit. The expected capacity might be 92 percent of the designed capacity. This concept is called *utilization* or *effective capacity*.

Effective capacity or utilization is simply the percent of design capacity actually expected. It can be computed by applying the following formula:

$$\textit{Utilization or effective capacity} \quad = \quad \frac{\textit{Expected Capacity}}{\textit{Design Capacity}}$$

Utilization or effective capacity is the maximum capacity that a company can expect to achieve given its product mix, methods of scheduling, maintenance and standards of quality. Another consideration is efficiency. Depending upon how facilities are used and managed, it may be difficult or impossible to reach 100 percent efficiency. Typically, efficiency is expressed as a percentage of the effective capacity. In calculating capacity, supervisors in a manufacturing sector need to take note of labor and equipment utilization, effectiveness and labor efficiency. Efficiency is a measure of actual output over effective capacity, as shown below:

$$Efficiency \quad = \quad \frac{Actual\ Output}{Effective\ Capacity}$$

Rated capacity is a measure of the maximum usable capacity of a particular facility. Without a knowledge of efficiency and utilization, rated capacity is impossible to compute. Rated capacity will always be less than or equal to the design capacity. The equation used to compute rated capacity is:

Rated Capacity = (Design Capacity) (Utilization) (Efficiency)

Although it is convenient to consider capacity planning as occurring in two main stages—namely, the determination of average levels and planning for meeting variations about this level—these two aspects are actually interdependent. The capacity provided might be influenced by the manner in which adjustments may be made. Constraints on adjustment, particularly limitations on ability to accommodate short-term excess demand may necessitate provision of excess capacity.

3.5 Manpower Needs

In essence, manpower planning is directed specifically to the size and composition of a work force of an organization. Supervisors are not only expected to manage their work force, but to be able to plan and forecast their future needs. There are three main issues that need to be dealt with in manpower planning. These are:

a. **Predicting.** Estimating (as precisely as possible) the manpower needs of the organization at some specific date in the future (i.e., January 1st next year), in terms of numbers, the various job categories and skills required; simultaneously estimating manpower supply at that future date based on present trends, identifying possible labor surpluses (overmanning) or labor shortage (vacancies) well in advance.

b. **Evaluating.** Working out the implications of the predictions in terms of action to be taken and the possible expense, as not only may more staff be needed but working space to accommodate them will be required as well.

c. **Controlling.** Making sure that the most effective use is made of available resources and that implementation of the plan proceeds in an orderly fashion.

Manpower planning is not easy. It can be costly when an organization begins to examine this technique. Even more difficult to estimate are possible changes in demand for products or services, even if the national economy changes as predicted. This is because (as an example) even high prices of energy hardly stops people from consuming vast quantities of it in houses and cars. Conversely, however, when the cost of postage goes up, there may be an immediate pronounced drop in mail traffic.

Organizations must try to become as efficient as possible in forecasting. The greater the experience level of the organization at forecasting, the more efficient they can become at it. They can then embark on the preparation of the manpower plan in the following stages:

Step 1	Identifying future needs
Step 2	Assessing the implications
Step 3	Assessing the present resources against future needs
Step 4	Ensuring that the target labor supply will be available
Step 5	Monitor and update regularly

There are great benefits to be obtained from manpower planning. It helps to review the present manpower levels and can reveal inefficiencies, overmanning and understaffing. Personnel can be recruited in good time. Redundancies can be anticipated or even avoided by redeployment or natural attrition. In addition to these, training programs and succession planning can be worked out in advance. Furthermore, the implications of changes, such as new resources required (lunchrooms, lockers, rest rooms, etc.), can be assessed, costed and provision made.

Predictions may not always be accurate and plans sometimes turn out to be inadequate, but this does not mean that it invalidates the whole technique. At worst, management will know where planning went wrong. Manpower planning is worth the effort. A "near miss" is better than no plan at all. Manpower planning is one that attempts to forecast the future demand for labor in an organization and formulates policies to ensure that as far as possible, the right number of each grade of staff is available when needed.

4
Recruitment

The aim of most organizations is to produce goods or services at a profit, or at least to break even. If the goods are to sell and the services to be demanded, then the people working in those organizations will need to be efficient in their jobs. Although people can be trained to do jobs, it is better from the start and makes training easier and simpler if people are placed in jobs to which their natural abilities and interests are reasonably suited.

From the supervisor's point of view, the process of filling vacancies is of great importance. After all, the supervisor will be responsible for newly recruited staff in the section, and not only for the initial training period but perhaps for years afterwards. Many supervisors have the good fortune to have a say in choosing their workers, and even those who do not will benefit from understanding some of the problems recruitment brings.

The terms *recruitment* and *selection* are often misused. Many people believe they are similar in meaning and that they cover the whole process of engaging personnel. *Recruitment* is properly used to cover the first stages of engaging personnel, namely:

a. The clarification of the exact nature of the job.

b. The sorting out of the skills, aptitudes and abilities required to do the job in question.

FIGURE 4.0

*The Recruitment and
Selection Process*

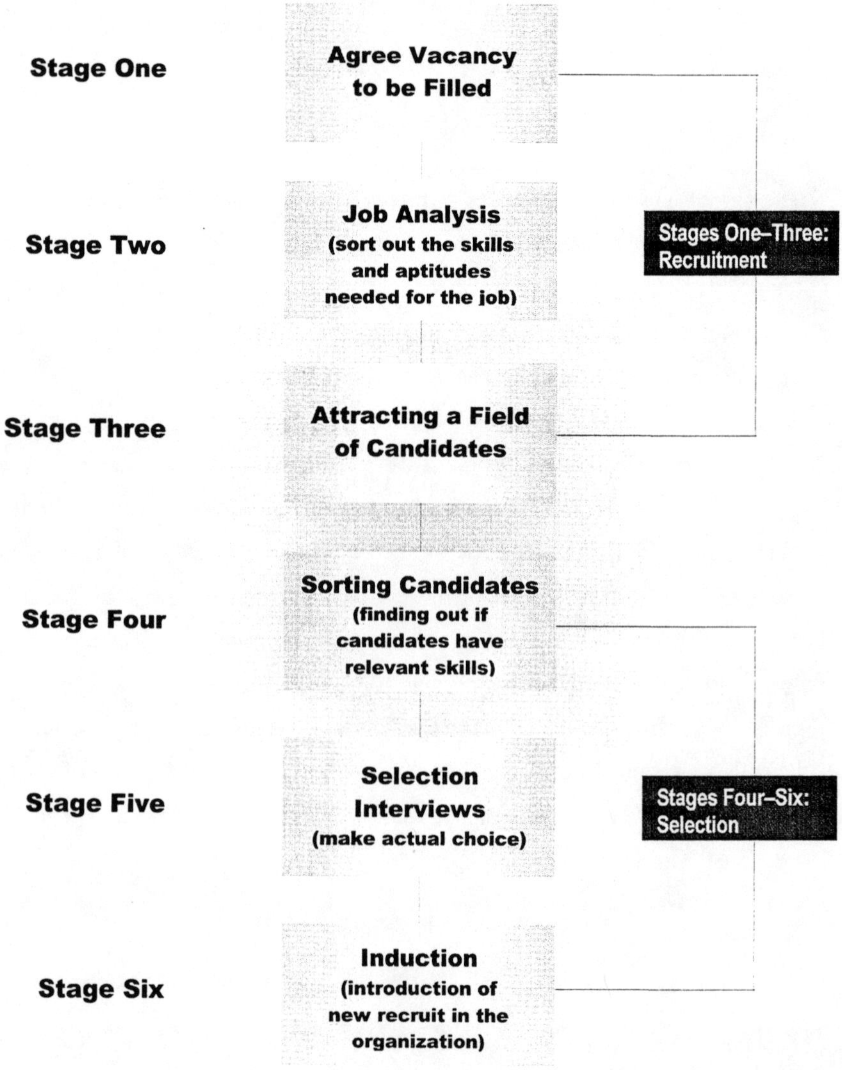

Stage One   **Agree Vacancy
to be Filled**

Stage Two   **Job Analysis**
(sort out the skills
and aptitudes
needed for the job)   **Stages One–Three:
Recruitment**

Stage Three   **Attracting a Field
of Candidates**

Stage Four   **Sorting Candidates**
(finding out if
candidates have
relevant skills)

Stage Five   **Selection
Interviews**
(make actual choice)   **Stages Four–Six:
Selection**

Stage Six   **Induction**
(introduction of
new recruit in the
organization)

c. The drawing up of a profile or "pen portrait" of the ideal candidate.

d. The attracting of a field of candidates by advertising or other means.

Selection is properly used to cover the later stages of engaging namely:

a. The sorting out of the total field of applicants into a sufficiently small "short list" for interview and possibly aptitude tests.

b. The selection interview stage, which leads to the ultimate decision to engage a particular candidate.

c. The induction process, which converts a successful candidate into a useful and cooperative worker.

The illustration (see *Figure 4.0*) on the previous page shows the distinction between these terms in diagrammatic form. It must be noted however that the recruitment and selection of individual employees should, of course, fit in with the overall manpower plan.

4.1 Job Specification

While the job description is a factual statement of the duties and responsibilities of a specific job, a job specification looks at the qualities that are required by a candidate to fit that job. In other words, a job specification is a further development of the job description and focuses on the qualities required by an individual ideally suited to a particular job. It is much more qualitative than the job description. Supervisory management employees assist the personnel or human resources department in the aspect of trying to marshal qualities that are considered necessary for success in a job under various categories, such as appearance, physique, personality, interest circumstances and career interests. Laws and regulations of many countries ban consideration of some factors, such as age, sex, race, national origin or religion.

A considerable number of job specifications used by many organizations are based upon the *Seven-Point Plan* of Alec Rodger or J. Munro Fraser's *Fivefold Grading System*. The following lists the categories found in both systems.

SEVEN-POINT PLAN (ALEC RODGER)

1. *Physical make-up:* Appearance, speech, health, etc.

2. *Attainments:* Education, training, experience, qualification

3. *General intelligence:* Intellectual capacity

4. *Special aptitudes:* Manual dexterity, verbal ability, literacy, numeracy

5. *Interests:* Intellectual, practical, social, artistic, sporting

6. *Disposition:* Steadiness, self-reliance, influence, acceptability

7. *Circumstances:* Family background, domestic circumstances

FIVEFOLD GRADING SYSTEM (J. MUNRO FRASER)

1. *Impact on others:* Appearance, speech, manner

2. *Acquired qualifications:* Education, training, experience

3. *Innate abilities:* "Brains," comprehension, aptitude for learning

4. *Motivation:* Level of objectives, determination, achievements

5. *Adjustment:* Emotional stability, ability to get on with others, to withstand stress

Both of the above methods provide a well-established and useful basis for a job specification, but it is not suggested that they should be slavishly followed. Each organization will need to adapt and develop its own method of specification in accordance with organizational needs and individual circumstances. The job specification completes the vitally important stage of analysis and criteria development of the recruitment process.

4.2 Internal/External Recruitment

Assuming that the need to fill a post has been established and justified, it will be necessary to review the supply side of the recruitment process. A popular practice is to divide the sources on an internal/external basis. The general principle of whether to recruit from within the organization or externally is often the subject of discussion and strong views may be held on this topic. What follows are the various sources of internal/external recruitment.

INTERNAL SOURCES

a. **Promotion.** In many cases, it may be possible to promote a subordinate or another employee within an organization to fill the vacant post. There are some companies that practice internal job postings, which are displayed on the notice boards to attract interested candidates internally. This should not present difficulties where a system of appraisal and staff development is in operation and it has obvious motivational advantages.

b. **Lateral "Sideways" Appointment.** It may be possible to transfer somebody of similar seniority from another department or area. Although this is sometimes frowned upon, it can help to develop and broaden the individual's experience and is often used as part of a management development program.

EXTERNAL SOURCES

The courses of external supply are, in theory, boundless, but in practice there are well-established methods of obtaining employees. The costs involved will vary and not all sources will be suitable for every job category. It is basically a question of "which source to choose" and experience will indicate the most suitable and appropriate source for filling a particular type of post. Some of the more common sources of supply are listed here.

a. **Direct Advertising.** This can have the advantage of reaching very large numbers of potential candidates but can also be very costly.

b. **Government Employment Agencies.** These include government job centers that serve those seeking work as well as employers looking for potential employees. There are specialist branches for youth employment and also a professional and executive recruitment service. They can be useful contacts, particularly with respect to local recruitment.

c. **Private Employment Agencies.** These are particularly useful for clerical staff and temporary jobs but there are also several specialist and executive agencies in business. A commission is typically charged for a successful match.

d. **Schools, Colleges and Universities.** Direct contact can be made with college career officers and career conventions are arranged at many universities. Many larger organizations recruit directly to fill their demand for young trainees and graduates.

e. **Introduction by Existing Staff.** Where vacancies are internally circulated, existing staff often recommend a friend or relative. This can be a fruitful source, as they are unlikely to recommend somebody who will not live up to their recommendation. In cases of mass employment, incentives are sometimes offered to encourage existing staff to recruit new employees.

f. **"Head-hunting."** Where a person of a particular talent or rare expertise is required, it may be necessary to search out somebody already in employment and induce him to change jobs. Although this practice is considered unethical in some quarters, it is generally accepted that it may be the only option open where a particular type of expertise is required.

There are all kinds of variations on the above themes and two or more methods can of course be used simultaneously. There are obvious occasions where it will be imperative to recruit externally. In circumstances where this is not the case, the advantages and disadvantages of external recruitment are basically the converse of those given above with respect to internal recruitment.

4.3 Advertising

Although many organizations have very good and useful relationships with schools and colleges as well as both public and private recruitment agencies, newspaper advertising is still a very popular way of recruitment. Economy is important in these days of rising costs but newspaper and magazine advertising can be a very effective method of attracting candidates. The aim of the job advertisement is to obtain an effective response at a reasonable cost. The main factors affecting this are the content of the advertisement and the timing of its appearance. Increasingly, some employers are advertising on the Internet or using web pages and other Internet resources to recruit employees.

Recruitment advertising, like any other form of advertising, is ideally dealt with by a specialist. The preparation and placement of an advertisement for maximum effect is something which many are prepared to attempt but at which few succeed. Larger personnel or human resources departments either employ their own experts or can afford to retain an advertising agency. However, there is no reason why the high costs of advertising should not be put to good effect, provided experience is used to supplement some basic ground rules such as:

a. Recruitment advertising should be aimed at an appropriate audience.

b. The advertisement should produce an adequate number of replies.

c. The contents should arouse interest and provide sufficient detail to prompt a response from the correct level of applicant.

A systematic method of processing these responses should be employed. It may be advisable to employ a control sheet in order to record what action has been taken with respect to each applicant. When an assessment has been completed, the "possible" candidates will usually be invited for interviews, and those who are considered unsuitable will be sent a letter that should leave them with a good impression despite any disappointment. The period

ELECTROSPACE INTERNATIONAL

Urgently requires a

SHIFT SUPERVISOR
($24,000 per annum)

The Job:

■ Responsible for daily production output
■ Supervise and retain a highly motivated work force
■ Coordinate and interface with other departments
■ Support cost improvement programs

The Requirements:

■ Diploma in production engineering/management
■ Minimum 3 years supervisory experience
■ Good oral and written communication in English
■ Able to perform rotating shift duties

Interested candidates should write in with detailed resume included to:

The Personnel Manager
Electrospace International
No. 2 Henderson Park, Singapore 0316

FIGURE 4.1

A Typical Advertisement

between the initial contact and a possible interview is crucial and delays or ambiguous communications could cause the loss of good candidates. An advertisement is only as good as the backup and follow-through that it receives.

4.4 Selection

The selection process takes over from the recruitment process once applications start being received. The first step is to compare the information provided by applicants with the personal characteristics detailed in the job specification, and to select a certain number of applicants considered to be probably or possibly suitable. Those selected will then be invited to attend interviews.

In many organizations, the initial sorting of applicants is done by the personnel or human resources department. The possible candidates are then handed over to the respective departments, who requested new employees for reviewing. Unless the post to be filled is a senior position, the interview will most likely to be conducted by the management having practical knowledge of the work to be performed, together with a personnel officer who attends to the paperwork involved. This is where supervisors play an active and important role as part of the recruitment process. They help in the decision of a suitable candidate for the job. Interviews are conducted in a cordial atmosphere; the whole exercise has to be conducted with one objective in mind—to find out how nearly does the applicant match, in skill, in experience, temperament and physical qualities, the "ideal" employee for such a job. However, no matter what the vacancy to be filled may be, no interview is to be carried out in an offhanded, casual or lighthearted manner.

Interviews for jobs like "Assistant Supervisor" or "Line-Leader" are usually conducted by a succession of people with each "sub-interview" being held at a different time. This is because these jobs are considered to be at supervisory level. Especially for supervisory or management posts, interviews are often conducted by two or three people, to reduce the effects of personal biases.

The proper planning of, and preparation for, interviews is essential for satisfactory and productive results. Supervisors conducting interviews need to refresh their memory by reading the appropriate job description and job specification. Then each application form with appropriate attachments, such as resumes, are read through carefully, and notes are made of specific questions that the supervisor may wish to ask the candidate during the interview. If the interviews are conducted by more than one person, a decision is usually reached regarding the order in which topics will be covered, not only to ensure that the interviews go smoothly but also to ensure that all forthcoming candidates receive equal and fair treatment. This is particularly important when both internal and external candidates are being interviewed for the same post in the same session. However, flexibility is also catered to as the varying personalities of different candidates would make rigid adherence to a plan counterproductive. Experienced supervisors conducting interviews would normally encourage candidates to talk and give information about themselves. This is because it will not be possible for the interviewer to assess the candidate's suitability or gain an impression of his character unless the candidate speaks up.

In many cases, a second interview of short-listed candidates may be used to supplement, but not to replace, the selection interview. For certain jobs, a selection test is necessary before a final selection is made. Tests that have been designed to show manual dexterity in simple tasks and those designed to test reasoning ability and to indicate the possession or lack of certain character traits are usually left to the qualified personnel or human resources department staff.

Once a final selection has been made of the candidate considered most suitable, the department that requires the candidate will inform the personnel or human resources department of its decision. It will then be left to the personnel or human resources department to offer the post to the successful candidate (including internal candidates). This is then followed by a letter of appointment that states, among other things, the date on which the candidate is to start work, the time at which the new employee should report and to whom. The letter will also state the terms and conditions of employment, such as hours of work, starting salary and other benefits, such as health insurance, vacation schedule, pension plan and educational benefits.

The interview and selection are not the end of the process as far as the successful candidate is concerned, and there is no way of being certain at that stage whether the most suitable or correct selection was made as only time will show that. The next step is induction—introducing the new employee to the organization—and training will be discussed in the following chapter of this study.

5
Training and Development

There is probably a greater awareness of the need for training and retraining at the present time than ever before. Apart from economic exigencies, the growth and sophistication of technology both now and in the future gives rise to a new dimension for the average career pattern. It is unlikely that anybody starting work at the present time will avoid a series of retraining periods to a greater or lesser extent. For an organization, a carefully planned but flexible program is vital if its work force is to be willing and able to accept the challenges that change will bring.

Employees must, therefore, be trained to acquire new skills to cope with new technology, and probably even more importantly, how to cope with change itself, be more adaptable and acquire attitudes sympathetic to change. Such training could be partially theoretical as well as practical, deal with the implications and potential of new equipment, be more "education" than training. Such training can be said to be "future-centered."

Finally, a way of tackling the problem of motivation is to try to cater to people's needs and ensure that their goals equate as far as possible with that of the organization. The work force, and individuals in general, will not be any different. They have goals and desires to develop abilities and talents and will want to satisfy their needs for self-realization. If management can help them to develop whatever potential these individuals may have, they may be able to make these employees more contented on the one hand, and have a use for their newly acquired skills in the future. Such training can be said to be "individual-centered."

5.1   Induction (Orientation) Programs

The primary objective of an induction (orientation) program is to give a newcomer an overview or overall appreciation of the organization that he or she has come into. Thus, the arrival of a new employee into an organization would set in motion the process called induction—that is, the process of introducing the employee to the enterprise, his job, the work group to which the employee will belong and the environment in which the employee will work. In some ways, induction could be considered a form of training as it includes familiarizing the newcomer with the work that the employee will actually perform.

The importance of a proper induction process is, unfortunately at times, overlooked by some organizations and management. The fact is that the quicker a newcomer settles in and "feels at home," and is accepted by and integrated with others in the work group, the quicker that person will be able to start performing the work the he or she was employed to perform. Whether the induction process is conducted by staff of the personnel or human resources department, a manager, a supervisor or a combination of two or more of them, it should be planned. First impressions gained by a newcomer about the work atmosphere and about the other members (of whatever status) of the work group are important, and can greatly influence the new employee. It is to be noted that new employees, especially those starting on their first jobs, are likely to be anxious and apprehensive. The induction program should therefore seek to put the new employee at ease as soon as possible.

The person who will probably be most intimately concerned with the job induction of a junior will be the supervisor in whose team the newcomer will work. The supervisor responsible for the job induction has the task of ensuring that the general knowledge gained by the newcomer is related to the individual tasks that are to be performed and the surroundings in which they are performed.

A supervisor who is delegated the responsibility for the job induction of a new employee must ensure that the newcomer knows the supervisor's name and how to contact him or her. If necessary, this information should be written down so that the new employee does not forget them. The supervisor must then ensure that the newcomer is aware of all facts concerning hours of work, meal break times and so on. The newcomer is usually shown around the department with emphasis on the section in which he or she will work, and on the location of entrances/exists, restrooms, lunchrooms, and safety/fire appliances. Where appropriate, the newcomer will also be shown where to obtain stationery, supplies, tools and other relevant materials.

The newcomer would be shown to his or her work location, and the work to be performed explained to the newcomer. Although the overall job may be explained, only some of the tasks involved may be concentrated upon to start. The location of machines or equipment that the employee may have to use is pointed out and the necessary instructions are given regarding operating equipment. Whether the new employees are adults or recent school graduates beginning their first job, their instructions always include talks on safety regulations, fire prevention and procedures in the event of an emergency.

It is to be noted, however, that the introduction of a new employee into an organization is not always easy. It must not be assumed that existing members of a work group will always welcome a newcomer with "open arms." Each member of the group will have his or her own character, temperament and agenda, and the supervisor (who will have the experience and knowledge of each person in the group) has to always take those differences into account when making introductions.

During the job induction period, the supervisor has to strike a delicate balance between guiding a new employee and leaving the employee alone from time to time to absorb knowledge on his or her own. A new employee must not be over-supervised, but at the same time must not feel isolated. To this end, supervisors need to encourage the newcomer to ask for assistance and guidance, the necessity for which should gradually grow less. An informal follow-up discussion with the new employee once a week for the first month or so is normally conducted to review progress. Should there be errors in the newcomer's work, the errors and how to avoid them in the future should be clearly explained. The discovery of an error is usually used by supervisors to give practical assistance and advice. This is because the establishment of a good working relationship between the supervisor and the subordinate is valuable in improving efficiency, productivity and loyalty.

Supervisors work together with the personnel or human resources department to monitor and review the progress of the new employee during the duration of the induction program. In some organizations "progress reports" on the performance of each new employee are prepared.

5.2 Supervisor's Role in Training

The supervisor, as a first line manager, plays a very important training role. We can identify two separate elements in such a role.

The first element is the training plan. The supervisor will contribute to the overall training plan. The appraisals he or she makes, the training needs he or she identifies, the recommendations he or she puts forward regarding particular individuals—all will be of considerable use. In addition, he or she may be entirely responsible for the on-the-job training in his department. He or she will then need to do all the initial work that is completed on an organization-wide scale on a smaller departmental scale, such as analyzing the work in the section, assessing the knowledge and abilities of his or her work force to do the work and creating a deficiency list as a basis for future training. The supervisor will have to consider future-centered training that could involve training chargehands—otherwise known as line-leaders in the electronics manufacturing industry—for permanent supervision or operators to move on to more complicated work. The supervisor's more intimate knowledge of his or her own work force can ensure that he or she will be aware of training needs and of its timing. In addition, the supervisor may be called upon to do some or all of the training in his or her department.

The second element is that of the supervisor as instructor. Before beginning any training or instructing, the supervisor needs to consider what learning, as opposed to teaching, is. Generally speaking, we may define learning as a "change in behavior made as a result of some past experiences." This allows for a very wide interpretation. A motorist who ignores a "yield" sign is summoned and fined. He learns the hard way not to repeat his error. A house-husband or -wife learns where the best shopping bargains are to be found and shops there.

However, this is an unreliable way of learning as the motorist who ignores road signs may never be caught and punished, but precisely directed training by a driving instructor could eliminate the driver's errors quite quickly. It is much the same with on-the-job training. If the supervisor leaves it to someone else, like an inexperienced worker, to show a newcomer what his or her job entails (or even leaves it to the newcomer to cope on his or her own), then this period will lead to less than satisfactory results. This is because it could very well end up being a lengthy session with possible misinformation communicated, which could lead to a high rate of initial errors. Moreover, it could lead to the teaching of unsafe and less efficient ways of doing jobs, as well as discouraging the newcomer. Therefore, precisely directed training is obviously needed.

The teaching of a skill is best considered in a series of steps. At all times during the process, the supervisor as an instructor should be prepared to answer all questions. The major elements of training are summarized below.

STEP 1. PREPARE THE TRAINER

The instructor must be thoroughly prepared. The instructor will need to know who he or she is to train, what the training objectives are, and the time available for the training. The instructor will also need to analyze and break down the job elements. This is done by listing each distinctive movement [remember *Motion Study*] or operation and highlighting key points, such as safety checks. The instructor will be required to have tools, safety equipment, training manuals and materials as well as a training checklist that lists relevant points to cover in a correct, logical manner.

STEP 2. PREPARE THE TRAINEE

Once the instructor is prepared and ready, he or she must next ensure that the trainee is ready to start learning. This is done by putting the trainee in a relaxed frame of mind. The instructor also needs to state very clearly exactly what the trainee is to learn. It would also be useful to find out how much (if any) knowledge the trainee has of the task that is to be taught.

STEP 3. DEMONSTRATE THE SKILL

The instructor now demonstrates the tasks or skill at normal speed once. He or she then proceeds to go through the task stage by stage slowly, making certain that the trainee knows exactly what is being done, how it is being done and the reason it is being done. The instructor repeats this stage as often as the particular instruction situation demands.

STEP 4. TRAINEE TO PRACTICE THE SKILL

The instructor gets the trainee to try the task himself, ensuring that the task is done slowly, and prompts the trainee to explain verbally as he or she goes along what is being done. During this step, the instructor would correct all errors as they are being made.

STEP 5. ASSIGNING TRAINEE TO PERFORM THE TASK

When *Step 4* is completed, the trainee begins on the normal task. Here, the instructor ensures that the trainee has not been assigned too high a target for beginning. The instructor also needs to be available to assist and guide the trainee at all times, as well as to check the trainee's work frequently.

Experience has shown that learning does not take place at a steady rate. Initial progress might be very slow, with sudden improvements, perhaps at totally unexpected times, followed by little additional progress for some considerable period. There will be a final leveling off when, without enormous effort, little further progress will be achieved. If one can plot learning progress on a graph, what is charted is called a *learning curve*, an example of which is shown in *Figure 5.0*. This graphic displays weekly plan set, the actual attainment and the ultimate goal of the standard output level to be reached.

The supervisor's role in training is to help develop the organizational training program by providing information on training needs of all levels of work in his or her department. In evaluating the training needs, the supervisor must ensure that it is cost effective, relevant and adequate.

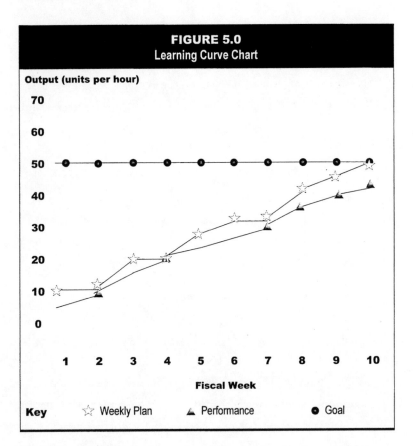

FIGURE 5.0
Learning Curve Chart

5.3 On-the-Job Training

On-the-job training (otherwise known as OJT) is a planned and organized program of training that is designed to meet the requirements of a definite objective, as opposed to incidental, haphazard training or training given for its own sake. The purpose of planned training is to bring a worker to a point where the worker can perform efficiently and safely in all aspects of the job to which he or she has been assigned or will need to be assigned. It should enable the worker to develop his or her greatest productive capacity, giving the worker simultaneously a sense of self-confidence and job satisfaction.

The term *on-the-job training* indicates the location where training actually takes place, rather than a type or method of training. In other words, OJT is given to an employee while the employee is productively engaged at his workstation. The vehicle of instruction is the material in the process of production or the task to be performed, together with the tools and equipment necessary for the production process or for the performance of the task. It may be the initial training for some employees, as is the case for a newcomer, while for others it may be an addition or supplement to preassignment training. It may be the only means of training for some, or it may be a supplement for off-the-job training (OTJ) for others. In either case, it takes place in a personal instructor-learner situation in which supervisors remain actively involved.

For supervisors to be effective in conducting on-the-job training for employees, they need to know what jobs must be done, the operations performed in each job and the elements workers need to learn in order to perform these operations. Thus, the supervisor needs to make a list of all jobs and operations performed by workers under his or her supervision in the work area. This can be done quite easily when the work is thoroughly and efficiently organized and broken down into specific jobs and operations; that is, when a complete analysis of the work area has already been made.

Every worker who is new to a job or whose duties and responsibilities are changed, and every worker who shows weakness in the performance of any job operation needs to be given on-the-job training. The job induction phase of orientation of a new worker is most effective when it is part of the initial OJT.

Supervisors also need to observe regular employees and appraise their work performance frequently. If an employee is not meeting production goals or standards of service, or if an employee is not adhering to safe and prescribed work methods and procedures, the causes should be studied to determine the training required. Supervisors have the responsibility of not allowing any worker to perform at a low level of performance. Every effort needs to be taken by the supervisor, as an instructor, to develop a subordinate through training.

For a well-rounded program, on-the-job training should be integrated with any *off-the-job training (Off-JT)* that is required to be given. Off-JT is a planned, organized job-related instruction given to an employee away from the physical workstation, usually in a group-classroom situation. The supervisor may assist the training department in conducting such classes. In developing a trainee into a skilled or semi-skilled worker, experience has shown that it is desirable to provide the worker with a minimum of one hour of planned off-the-job instruction for every ten hours of on-the-job training. In some cases, however, this ratio of Off-JT to OJT could be higher. For instance, the training of waiters or waitresses normally requires a higher ratio of Off-JT to OJT since training cannot be given in front of guests.

Training such as OJT and Off-JT more than pays for itself through the elimination of the hidden costs of lowered productivity, which are inevitable when learning is an accidental, trial-and-error process.

6
Communication

In the past, whenever an organization had problems with people, the management looked immediately at conditions of work, pay, incentives and other such practical applications. Today, more emphasis is placed on the relationships of people with each other and their various attitudes and feelings. Difficulties within such relationships are often ascribed to "a failure of communication."

A failure of communication does not simply mean that people do not, or cannot, talk to each other. This, of course, may be true sometimes and it may be necessary for management of all levels, including supervisors, to look deeper into the attitudes of the employees and find out why there is no communication taking place at all. More often, however, it means that people do talk to each other, telephone each other, write to each other, but somehow still cannot understand each other. Communication is two-way and is primarily concerned with understanding. It is the way in which one individual passes on a message, an instruction, information, question or idea from his mind to the mind of another person. If communication is to be successful, a message must be received without being altered, confused or misunderstood.

Such a process sounds simple enough. In practice it is very difficult (especially in a large organization) for, however well we plan a communication and however hard we try to consider the recipient, there are many pitfalls that may trap us as we try to put our message across.

6.1 Communication and People

The starting point must be to consider what happens between people when they are communicating and to examine the lines of communication that exist in an organization. This is fundamental to an understanding of why it is so important to have good communication. As far as supervisors are concerned, communication means interaction with people. Although mechanical means, such as telephones, computers, fax machines and copiers are used in transmitting information, these are still only machines and do not have voices or feelings. People do. Thus, when supervisors communicate, they have to think about the human beings with whom they are talking or to whom they are writing.

Supervisors, in the course of their work, communicate with their subordinates, counterparts in other departments as well as their immediate supervisors and, at times, with higher management. There is a great deal of information that is required to be disseminated. Therefore, supervisors need to understand the barriers to communication. The following summarizes these:

a. **Relationships between People.** The attitudes, actions and reactions of people to each other can impede or even prevent communication.

b. **Language.** The words that we use may not be understood, may be misunderstood, or may hold different meanings. Each individual's background knowledge affects the understanding of a message.

c. **Listening.** An inability or unwillingness to listen effectively will reduce an individual's ability to comprehend and retain information.

d. **Systems.** Messages will often not reach the people who need information correctly and speedily if there are no effective formal systems of communication.

In organizations where there is no effective formal communication system, it is common to find a very strong informal channel reaching into every level, which is commonly called "the grapevine" or "the bush telegraph." This informal channel spreads rumor and gossip very rapidly. It is, however, very unreliable because, although each rumor might have originally contained a grain of truth, it will have become distorted or magnified through its passage from one person to another until it is almost unrecognizable. The grapevine can never be completely eradicated. The most that can be done is to reduce its influence by making full and correct information available to the right people at the earliest possible time.

Management may sometimes use the grapevine deliberately—for instance, to ascertain staff reactions to possible changes before putting them forward as firm proposals. Front line supervisors, who are often the link between management and direct operating staff, need to be discreet and careful so that staff do not realize what is being done, so that the meaning of the message is not changed radically. This can be a dangerous course of action and extreme caution needs to be exercised—there are many more reliable and better ways of uncovering what the work force thinks and wants.

6.2   Channels of Communication

Every organization needs to develop an effective system of communication. The more complex an organization is, the more complex the communication systems that are needed. The simplest analysis of the systems of communication is that which considers a three-way flow—downward, upward and horizontal.

Downward communication comes from the management levels. It sometimes originates at the top and goes down as far as middle management, sometimes further. At other times, it originates at a lower level and reaches the ordinary worker. Downward communication tends to consist of either instruction or information. The instruction may take the form of orders, or may be more politely phrased as requests and suggestions. The flow of information is often of a more general nature than are instructions. Much of the information will be appropriate and useful, though some of the items will be unnecessary and time-wasting. For instance, an abstract of production forecasts fed through the computer might be useful to a supervisor but the supervisor would be unlikely to have the time to plow through the detailed computer printout, which comprises twenty or more sheets of figures.

Horizontal communication is the flow of information between people who are at the same level in an organization—for example, between members of the workplace or between supervisors in a manufacturing department. With the growth of large-scale organizations, the desirability of improving horizontal communication has become a necessity. The increased use of specialist departments alone illustrates this. To facilitate horizontal communication, meetings are held to allow personal contact among staff.

Upward communication is most frequently used in the case of employee/ employer consultation, enabling workers to present views and discuss problems with management. Supervisory staff actively participate in this feedback mechanism. Within individual departments of an organization, upward communication exists on a casual day-to-day basis and is often very successful. It is, however, sometimes lacking elsewhere in the management structure. Such a lack is often felt by junior management to be a refusal by senior executives to recognize the contributions that more junior personnel could make.

The above, of course, is a very simplified description. There are very many other ways in which communication may flow and whichever system is used, there will be effects on the patterns of behavior of the people within that system. For example, in a formal meeting each speaker will address the chair of the meeting but what the supervisor says will be heard by all the other members of the meeting. They will each react to the speaker's words.

The behavior of the meeting attendees will also be very much affected by the way in which the chair responds to the remarks made. Supervisors who conduct meetings need to have a firm grasp on these issues and have to learn to act accordingly. Whatever the systems in an organization are, and however good they may appear in theory, it is evident that they will still fail to be effective if the relationships between people are not good. The breakdown of the systems can mean that communication completely or partially ceases, or it can mean that people seek different ways of communicating, outside the prescribed system.

6.3   The Unions and Staff Associations

Very many organizations have members who belong to labor unions. Others have staff associations. Systems of communication must exist between management and such bodies and must be so organized that communication with them is effective but does not adversely affect the normal communication flow within the organization. Management must ensure that communication downward reaches all levels and understand that it is not possible, for instance, for the production worker to learn of a proposed change from his shop floor steward before the supervisor knows about it. Also, employees must be encouraged to talk to their supervisors about problems and suggestions rather than always going first to their union representative.

This is not to say that there should be any attempt to deny to the union or staff associations full opportunities for consultation and discussion on matters affecting both groups and individuals. Rather, it is a recognition that there are some things that are appropriately channeled through the union, while others should not be. At the very simplest level, if a production operator has an equipment or machine problem, one would expect her to report the problem to her supervisor, not to her union. Conversely, however, there should always be a place for union involvement in any grievance procedure.

6.4 Supervisors as Communicators

In this section, common situations faced by supervisors in which communication plays a vital part will be examined. Supervisors, in their line of work, give orders and instructions as well as conduct interviews and handle grievances. As meetings intrude more and more on the supervisor's time, this aspect of communication has also become important.

For many supervisors, verbal communication is by far the most frequently used medium. This is because face-to-face communication has many advantages. Such advantages include:

a. Ability to alter presentation to suit receiver

b. Subtleties of tone and stress

c. Facial expressions, which can help convey meaning

d. Availability of feedback

However, there are times when written communication is in fact preferable. When there are instructions to manufacture products or to provide specifications, parts numbers or any complex or complicated mass of information, written communication is the preferable method. Staff who work on different shifts, especially those working the night shift, rely heavily on written communication. This is highly evident in the electronics manufacturing sector, where production supervisors on shift duty use communication books to transmit messages to their counterparts.

The distinction between an order and an instruction is rather fine. There are many occasions where the two words are virtually interchangeable in everyday use. The order can be regarded as a simple direction to do something, whereas the instruction is an order plus an explanation of how the job is to be done. Supervisory staff usually deal with various types of orders and instructions. These are briefly outlined on the following pages.

a. **The Direct Order.** Written orders tend to be of this type. It is a one-way communication to get something done quickly, when the receiver knows exactly what to do. Supervisors need to be cautious about using commands as they do not only assume knowledge on the part of the worker, but a sensitive person may feel antagonized. A supervisor who is always giving direct orders runs the risk of creating both uncertainty and ill will, and may find himself or herself in an awkward position if he or she has to give a worker detailed instructions after a command. In the work environment, such direct orders or commands are best left to emergency situations, such as fire drills.

b. **The Appeal.** This type of order is softer, a request rather than a command, and it helps to reduce the receiver's resistance to a minimum by arousing an air of cooperation. Supervisors who use this approach treat people in a courteous and friendly way, as well as play down the superior-subordinate relationship. However, like the command, it assumes that the recipient of the order knows quite a lot about the job and detailed instructions are not required.

c. **The Hint.** This is the mildest type of order. Here, supervisors need to just mention the subject, sometimes in a very oblique way, to an experienced and reliable worker who knows what is wanted without instructions. Sometimes this type of order is referred to as an *implied order*.

d. **The Open Order.** This is one in which supervisors announce a piece of information, such as, "I'm afraid it looks like we have to complete the inventory count by the weekend." Usually this information sets a target, but again, no instructions on how the job is to be done are given. It leaves the subordinate free to use initiative in carrying out the task.

e. **Signing or Taking the Initiative.** These are non-verbal methods of giving orders. An example would be a supervisor who says, "We had better clear this lot," and then begins to do the job himself. This method is useful where there are workers whose command of English is limited, or where there are people who are reluctant to do a job in a certain way or feel the job cannot be done in that particular way.

f. The Detailed Order (Instructions). Giving people job instructions is very much like training people. The only difference is that untrained staff need a more careful and longer instruction period. So the giving of instructions is, in effect, a modified form of teaching. The implication is, therefore, that one uses a strategy similar to a training approach.

6.4.1 Interviews and Handling Grievances

An interview is essentially an exchange of information, ideas or opinions between two or more persons. In that sense it is no different from thousands of other instances of communication that occur in a day. However, an interview is different for the following reasons:

a. It is communication for a particular purpose.

b. It is conducted with a greater amount of privacy.

c. One participant (the interviewer) takes the lead and, in theory, controls the course the interview takes.

There are many different types of interviews. The most important include recruitment, coaching, induction, instruction, appraisal (a discussion of an employee's progress), disciplinary and also interviews dealing with grievances, requests or suggestions coming from the employee. Interviews take many different forms, and it is difficult to acquire a universal guide. In-house training by some organizations on how to conduct an interview follow basic points. These basic guidelines are:

a. Keeping interviews as private as circumstances allow.

b. Choosing surroundings that are free of noise and distraction.

c. Whatever the reason for the interview, normal politeness and courtesy is important.

d. Both interviewer and interviewee must sit on the same level.

e. Plan the interview in advance.

f. Listen as well as talk.

g. Sum up the interview at the end, to ensure that the interviewee understands what (if anything) has been agreed upon.

One of the most critical interviews that supervisors have to tackle is the disciplinary interview. These are usually equally despised by both supervisors and workers, and for that reason are often avoided. However, failure to act can only lead to increasing trouble as time passes and result in steady erosion of the control a supervisor should have in a department. *The Employment Act* in many countries often requires a statement of the stages in disciplinary proceedings be included in the contract of employment. Thus, all employers must have a definite procedure, of which the supervisor must be fully aware. The limits to the supervisor's powers to discipline are very important.

Another important aspect of a supervisor's job is the handling of grievances at the workplace. A grievance is a feeling in the back of an employee's mind that there is something in the work situation that the worker feels is wrong, unjust, unfair or reasonable as far the worker is concerned. It follows, therefore, that while some grievances are genuine and well founded, others are less well founded, or even imaginary. However, they must all be treated seriously. As with disciplinary matters, the law mandates that information on grievance-making be given to employees at the time of their employment by the organization. Such procedures are usually negotiated between management and union, and consist of a series of agreed-upon steps. The aim is to prevent an individual grievance being left unresolved and gradually growing until it becomes a grievance of all workers and a subject of a dispute.

Following on the last point, it is obvious that the supervisor cannot always wait for grievances to be raised officially. The supervisor must know his workers sufficiently well to appreciate when something seems to be "bugging" them. A change from the normal behavior is a possible indicator—the willing worker who virtually "works to the rule," the person who normally takes care and pride in his or her work and now does what he or she has to do in an indifferent or even careless way. At this stage it becomes important for the supervisor to act quickly.

6.4.2 Meetings

Meetings normally involve two or more people and are called for a specific purpose. They are often publicized beforehand and are either formal or informal in character. Meetings are generally not popular but they are growing in size, frequency and length. It is clear we pay considerable attention to meetings these days; for example, when industrial disputes arise in any country and threaten to disrupt its economy, it is viewed on television. The supervisor, therefore, cannot escape attending meetings called by others and the supervisor may have to call them himself. It is important, then, that every supervisor knows what is expected of him or her both as a member and as a leader of meetings.

In industry or commerce, it is not practical to run meetings according to formal procedures, as they are very rigid. If anything is to be achieved, ideas, positive thinking and purposeful problem-solving must be encouraged at meetings. At less formal industrial meetings, one should let the needs of the situation dictate the form of the meeting and the rules, customs and practices that are normally followed.

The duties of the chair or discussion leader of a meeting are to keep order, keep the agenda on track, conduct the session according to procedures (if it is a formal meeting), and see that the opinions of the majority are clearly recorded. He or she also has to resolve any deadlocks. The chairman has to ensure that the minutes of the meeting are recorded. Minutes of record report the topics discussed, who proposed and seconded motions, the working of the motion and the result of the vote on the motion taken at the meeting. Minutes of narration are more likely to be seen by a supervisor. These minutes are a shortened record of what everyone said on each topic at the meeting, including arguments for and against, promises made, undertakings given. These are invaluable later as a reference to see who agreed to do what.

As discussed, the supervisor's role may be as a meeting member or as a discussion leader. This is because, as stated earlier, a supervisor in the course of his work gets called to meetings by others and may be required to call meetings himself or herself.

The supervisor as a meeting member. If meetings are to be effective, every member, including the supervisor, should be on time because being late wastes everyone else's time. Every member needs to be adequately prepared, which means reading the agenda (if there is one) beforehand, and bringing along records and other appropriate documents. Members must concentrate on solving problems instead of winning arguments. They need to be objective and willing to compromise. To be useful, all arguments put forward must be supported by facts.

The supervisor as chair (discussion leader). If the supervisor as discussion leader is to get the best out of a meeting and its members, the supervisor should:

a. Be adequately prepared. He or she should know the objective of the meeting, have as many facts available as possible, see that agendas are issued to members and, if necessary, see people beforehand to go over with them the particular contributions that they are to make.

b. Make clear what is being discussed so as to eliminate any irrelevant discussion.

c. Steer the discussion. Help members to continue with the discussion by interjecting questions and making points when other members are reluctant to intervene.

d. Try to get everyone to participate.

e. Summarize the discussion at intervals. This is useful because it reminds meeting attendees of what has been said or agreed upon already. A final summary should be made at the end of the meeting.

f. Make certain members understand what they have agreed to do.

g. Get as much agreement on each topic as possible. It is poor chairmanship to let a discussion wander on without reaching any conclusion.

h. Avoid being autocratic. This can be seen in chairs who are full of their own ideas, give too many opinions of their own and cut short any opposing ideas.

i. If a meeting is a failure or does not achieve the desired results, the supervisor (as chair) should always ask himself what went wrong and was the fault his? An appraisal of the meeting should be done to review possible flaws that could be corrected in future meetings.

7

Morale and Motivation

In a manufacturing organization, supervisors are usually assessed on their productivity performance. Apart from leadership and management skills, productivity is an important indicator of a supervisor's capability.

Productivity is one of those terms which, at first glance, seems rather obvious, but which becomes very difficult to put one's finger on when an exact definition is required. In most cases, in general, any employee action that improves and furthers management objectives can be described as productivity. For decades, business leaders and management consultants on human resources development have had an abiding faith in the inevitable relationship of morale and productivity. At first glance, this relationship seems simple and implies a high degree of causality in its logic.

The theory is that if one increases the capability of the job situation and the working environment to satisfy the manifest needs of the workers, morale increases and the motivation of workers to continue in that environment and gratify their needs similarly increases. It follows that this increase in motivation results almost automatically in a higher degree of productivity—everything else being equal—since most of us subscribe to the theory of the equation:

$$\text{MOTIVATION} \times \text{ABILITY} = \text{PERFORMANCE}$$

Morale is thus viewed as the signal of a motivating job situation. By this reasoning, anything one does that increases the morale of an organization should also increase productivity. Unfortunately, from the point of view of both the businesspersons and the behavioral theorists, evidence has been accumulating that indicates that the relationship between morale and productivity is far more complex than had been previously assumed.

Indeed, there is a strong possibility that if a relationship between morale and productivity exists at all, the causality may be in the reverse direction. That is, organizations with both high morale and high productivity may have the high morale because they *are* productive. The best way to increase morale may be to facilitate those factors in the job situation—particularly supervisory quality, quantity and style—that have been shown to have the greatest direct effects on productivity. Since this concept represents a significant departure from traditional management theory, it would be useful to examine the various components of the morale-productivity relationship to explore the evidence.

7.1 Morale, Job Satisfaction and Productivity

Morale is a collective, abstract characteristic. The term refers to the state of mind of a group of employees. In a way, it is their collective attitude towards their work, management and the conditions that define their relationship to the organization to which they belong. On the other hand, it may have components that have nothing whatsoever to do with the work situation. Common factors may include the employee's home environment, socioeconomic pressures and other similar variables, which all have their effects on the job-related attitudes of the individual worker as well as upon the morale of the entire work force of the organization.

While remaining a convenient subject for discussion, morale has been replaced in management research literature by a somewhat narrower concept of job satisfaction. The dimension of job satisfaction has been under investigation for many years. In the research conducted, the job satisfaction variables that have emerged show a high degree of constancy. The following appear to be the commonly cited dimensions:

a. The contents of the work, actual tasks performed and the control of work

b. Characteristics of direct supervision

c. The organization and its management

d. Opportunities for advancement

e. Salary and other financial benefits

f. Coworkers

g. Working conditions

The distribution of these factors and their relative importance to the overall satisfaction differ from situation to situation and with the occupational levels of workers. However, it is also a fact that most groups of workers have common job satisfaction goals. We are thus able to characterize human motives leading to the classification of these goals into two main groups. One is the *physical maintenance* and the other is the *psychological growth motive.*

Much has been written in recent years regarding this dual aspect of human motivation. In the business area, this is represented by works like McGregor's "THEORY X AND THEORY Y," Herzberg's two-factor theory of "MOTIVATION HYGIENE" and McClelland's "NEED FOR ACHIEVEMENT" theory. Although these theories differ in their details, they all have a dual set of motives. On the one hand, every individual tries to maintain comfortable physical condition, avoiding pain and discomfort, and to achieve stability for the long-term. On the other hand, the individual strives to fulfill his or her inherent potentials and capabilities and experience the satisfaction that comes from successfully accomplishing a challenging task.

Studies have shown beyond doubt that morale and, in particular, job satisfaction are measurable human characteristics that are important to individuals in their line of work. As such, it would be reasonable to say that job satisfaction used as a goal should be able to determine the job performance behavior to a certain degree. However, it would be disastrous to assume that by correlating the measure of job satisfaction and productivity alone, one finds a systematic relationship. This is because a comprehensive study has recently shown that the only production-oriented factor that had a consistent and significant relationship to measures of job satisfaction was employee turnover. Although other factors are not entirely devoid of relationship to job satisfaction, the study merely represents that no simple statement can be made from it. A pertinent point that needs to be considered is the relationship between job satisfaction and supervision.

7.2 Effects of Direct Supervision

Many of the more complex studies of job satisfaction have been aimed at supervision as the major satisfaction-determining variable. Most of the studies find that supervisory behaviors and practices affected employee attitudes and were related to the performance criteria on both group and individual bases. This tends to reflect the complexity of the supervisor-subordinate relationship and its effect on both productivity and morale. There are three attributes of supervision, in general, that are important to the job satisfaction and work efficiency link. These are:

a. Encouragement of efficiency and productivity

b. Going to bat for subordinates

c. Power to reward

These attributes, however, do not bear simple relationships to productivity. For example, if **(a)** and **(b)** are both high, then efficiency is high; but if **(a)** is high and **(b)** is low, efficiency is low. Furthermore, both grievances and turnover tend to be higher if the supervisor's desire for high productivity exceeds the supervisor's consideration of employee welfare. This shows that the interactions of these attributes is an important factor to note. A high degree of supervisory consideration for subordinates **(b)** will to some extent compensate for a high desire for productivity **(a)**, but a low valuation of consideration will not compensate for a lack of desire for productivity.

Again, we see the complexity of the interrelationship between morale and productivity, which is a key factor of measurement for supervisory staff, as stated earlier. On the one hand, job satisfaction is very heavily influenced by those psychological factors dependent upon supervisory style; and on the other hand, the productivity of a work group is similarly affected by supervision. This might lead us to the conclusion that morale and productivity are directly related, when in fact they are both dependent upon the action of a third variable. There is the possibility that job satisfaction is contingent upon satisfactory performance and is directly mediated by the quality of supervision. This means that in order to increase both morale and productivity, it is necessary to operate on the connecting link between the two—that is, the supervisor.

7.3   Work Environment

The work environment that is to be discussed here reflects more the psychological rather than the physical environment. The physical environment must be constituted in such a way that the employee has the necessary equipment, workstation, lighting and atmospheric conditions that enable employees to work efficiently and in reasonable comfort. There is little evidence from the behavioral sciences that improving the physical environment beyond this point can motivate a worker to perform better.

But if the physical environment does not serve as a motivator, it *can* serve very well as a demotivator. A bad environment can lessen performance through inadequate facilities. That is, the worker simply does not have the tools to perform efficiently. A poor physical environment can demotivate an employee in the sense that it conveys a lack of concern by management.

Moving on to the next level, we can show that better production can be accomplished with the same amount of worker motivation by modifying work procedures. That is, we take a given level of energy directed at work and, by utilizing it more efficiently, gain greater productivity. If the work situation is properly designed, it can help support these procedures. The physical environment simply reflects an analysis of the workflow.

Psychological research has shown that the redesign of work procedures and the consequent modification of the production environment must be consistent with worker expectations if they are to be accepted. Almost any change, no matter how drastic, will be accepted if there is no alternative. But, of course, there always is an alternative—that is, the employee can leave! So if changes are to be made, they must be in the direction of providing greater job satisfaction. However, it must be remembered that procedural efficiency is of little avail if it is obtained at the cost of decreasing the "fun" of the job. The increase in job satisfaction obtained by making jobs more complex or increasing responsibility may very well reduce turnover to the point where management can afford to ignore the industrial engineering bias, which automatically assumes that job restructuring that departs from optimum engineered standards results in decreased efficiency.

Finally, we can most directly improve productivity and morale by directly increasing the effectiveness of front line management staff. There is a developed set of prescriptions for the high producing supervisor. This supervisor is viewed by subordinates as:

a. The supervisor is supportive, friendly and helpful rather than hostile.

b. The supervisor shows confidence in subordinates, which leads the supervisor to have high expectations of their performance.

c. The supervisor sees to it that subordinates are well trained. The supervisor helps them get promoted or upgraded.

d. The supervisor coaches and assists employees whose performance is below the acceptable standard.

e. The supervisor is a leader who develops subordinates into a working team with high group loyalty by using effective group leadership practices.

While morale or, more properly, job satisfaction, can be reliably measured and its dimensions accurately described, it can be only modestly related to most measures of productivity—and then only through the mediation of supervision. The one exception appears to be the strong relationship between low morale and turnover.

It is, however, possible to achieve good morale and high productivity by improving the psychological environment through the medium of job satisfaction and upgrading supervisory quality and quantity. The greatest return on investment in achieving better worker morale, reducing turnover and increasing productivity can be obtained by first modifying the psychological environment, next the procedural environment, and last the physical environment.

7.4   Goal-Setting and Path Improvement

Goal-setting plays a central role in the goal path process. It is the establishment of targets and objectives for successful performance, both long range and short range. It provides a measure of how well individuals and groups are meeting performance standards set by management. As front line leaders, supervisors represent top management in setting goals and monitoring them.

The theory underlying goal-setting is that human behavior is goal-directed. Group members need to feel that they have a worthwhile goal that can be reached with the resources and leadership available. Without goals, different members go in different directions. This difficulty will continue as long as there is no common understanding of the goals involved. The goal setting process requires at least four steps: define the goals, set specific goals, make the goals challenging and give consistent feedback about goal accomplishment.

Goal Definition. Proper goal definition requires a supervisor to explain clearly the purpose behind the goals and the necessity for them. Whatever the situation, people need goals that are meaningful to them in order to be fully motivated.

Specific Goals. Goals need to be as specific as possible so that employees will know when a goal is reached. It is not enough to say, "Do your best," because that kind of goal is not specific enough for most people. In other words, the goal must be measurable so that it can be appraised without difficulty.

Goal Difficulty. Somewhat surprisingly, most employees work harder when they have difficult goals to accomplish than easy ones. Difficult goals present a challenge that appeals to the achievement motive within employees.

To obtain commitment to difficult goals, however, supervisors typically invite employees to participate in the goal-setting process. In this way, employees make a conscious commitment to achieving the goal.

Feedback about Progress toward Goal. When people have well-defined goals, they need feedback about how well they are reading their goals. Otherwise, they feel "lost" and have no way of knowing how successful they are. For example, a football team needs to know its score if the team members are to remain motivated; the same could be said for a team on a production line. Job feedback tends to encourage better job performance, and self-generated feedback is a very powerful motivational tool.

The steps surrounding goal-setting represent only half of the path-goal process. Supervisors also need to consider some contingency factors, such as employee personality characteristics and the nature of the task, before deciding how to go about smoothing the path towards a goal. Supervisors provide both task and psychological support for their employees. They provide task support when they help assemble the resources, budgets and other elements that are essential to get the job done. Equally important, they can remove environmental constraints that sometimes inhibit employees, exhibit upward influence and provide recognition upon effective efforts and performance. But psychological support is also needed. Supervisors must stimulate people to want to do the job. The supervisor must be able to give employees the recognition that their work is important. In this way, employees will get the feeling that they are working together with the supervisor to get the entire job done.

It is often said that supervisors tend to supervise as they are supervised. They serve as role models, or examples, for their subordinates, who tend to act in about the same way that the supervisors do. For example, if a supervisor is considerate and supportive with his or her subordinates, the subordinates' responses are likely to be similar. However, if a supervisor exhibits an opposing behavior, employees will probably react accordingly.

7.5 Performance Appraisals

Performance appraisals play a key role in reward systems. It is the process of evaluating the performance of employees. As shown in *Figure 7.0*, appraisal is necessary in order to:

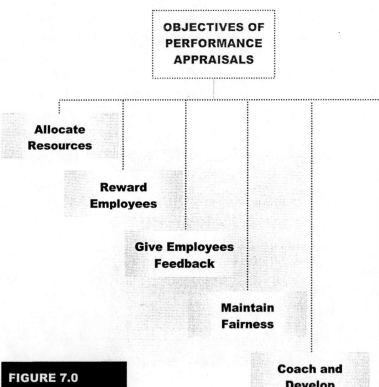

OBJECTIVES OF PERFORMANCE APPRAISALS

Allocate Resources

Reward Employees

Give Employees Feedback

Maintain Fairness

Coach and Develop Employees

Comply with Equal Opportunity Regulations

FIGURE 7.0

Objectives of Performance Appraisals

a. allocate resources in a dynamic environment

b. reward employees

c. give employees feedback about their work

d. maintain fair relationships within groups

e. coach and develop employees

f. comply with regulations

Appraisal systems are therefore necessary for proper management and employee development.

Supervisors regularly make important decisions on employee pay, promotion, transfer, job training and continued employment with the organization. Usually, these decisions are based on solid information that is systematically obtained and carefully considered. At times, however, supervisors make recommendations based on a somewhat unreliable memory of past events or a dramatic recent occurrence. Making judgments about employees is not the same as performance appraisal. Judgments have a "spur of the moment" quality to them. The judgments may very well be accurate. But, just as likely, they can be grossly unfair to the individual being judged. To reduce the chances of making inaccurate judgments about employee performance, most organizations use some form of performance appraisal. The factors typically evaluated include: quantity and quality of work, job knowledge, timeliness of completion, cost effectiveness, amount of supervision required, attendance, judgment and leadership potential.

There are several purposes and benefits of performance appraisals. These are outlined below.

Get the Doubt Out. Clearing up uncertainty is one purpose of the performance appraisal. The very process of taking time to talk about performance gives the subject special status. The message to the employee is clear.

Because supervisors have to meet face-to-face with their employees, supervisors are forced to be prepared to state their feelings about future performance. This process allows employees the opportunity to raise questions, resolve doubts and give suggestions.

Shape Behavior. The appraisal process simultaneously encourages and discourages certain types of employee behavior. Knowing what is expected and rewarded draws employees in that direction. Supervisors who give appropriate "praises and raises" encourage employees along the way. On the other hand, the wrong behavior is quickly spotted and discouraged.

Make Better Personnel Decisions. Having better information on the employee's performance means that the supervisor and the organization will make sounder decisions on such matters as pay, transfers, promotions, job training and continued employment.

Supervisor's Understanding Improved. The review process forces supervisors to think about each individual's performance and connection to the total department. Because the process is ongoing rather than hit or miss, supervisor and employees come to learn what does and does not work with each employee. Future assignments are geared with certain insights.

Convert Employee Potential to Actuality. For most people, job motivation is a fragile thing. They bring their high hopes and expectations to the job. But far too often, past experiences have shown that organizations fail to encourage the development of that potential. Performance appraisal makes it easier, and it can even be automatic for the organization to express concern for employee development, create individualized plans for upgrading and lead employees down the path to their development and progression with the organization.

Improved Performance is Contagious. As individual performance improves, the effect catches on with others. They do not want to be outdone, so in turn they try harder.

Employees are Protected. As performance expectations are spelled out, everyone knows what is required. If the employees meet performance expectations, they have every right to feel secure in their jobs. Of course, there is no way to give employees total job security, as business conditions can cost jobs regardless of how well individuals perform. The chances of being let go for personality conflicts or incomplete information on performance are, however, greatly reduced.

The performance appraisal is widely accepted by both employees and management. Managements see appraisals as one of the tools to use to tell employees what to do to get along on the job and how well they are doing in relation to those guidelines given. Generally speaking, performance reviews help supervisors to become more effective as they spend more time observing employees and realize how certain suggestions or ideas will help the employees do better work. Through this vehicle, management is able to improve morale and motivation in an organization.

8
Counseling

Counseling is discussion of a problem that usually has emotional content with an employee in order to help the employee cope with the issue better. Counseling seeks to improve employee mental health. Good mental health means that people feel comfortable about themselves, positive about other people and are able to meet the demands of life.

The definition of counseling implies a number of characteristics. It is an exchange of ideas and feelings between two people—a counselor and a counselee—so it is an act of communication. Since it helps employees cope with problems, it should improve organizational performance because the employee is more cooperative, worries less about personal problems or improves in other ways. Counseling also helps the organization be more human and considerate to people problems.

In a manufacturing organization, supervisors act as counselors on the production floor. In situations where job stress or personal problems prevail, supervisors counsel their staff to help them reduce stress. Counseling is usually confidential so that employees will feel free to talk openly about their problems. It involves both work-related and personal problems because both types of problems affect an employee's performance on the job. Although a few companies had employee counseling programs at an earlier date, the recognized beginning of employee counseling was in 1936 at Western Electric Company in Chicago. It is believed that this was the first time a company used the term *personnel counseling* for employee counseling services. Employee job satisfaction definitely improved as a result of the counseling.

8.1 Functions of Counseling

The need for counseling can arise from a variety of employee problems. When these problems exist, employees benefit from understanding and help of the type that counseling can provide. For example, an employee is hesitant to take the risk required by promotion, so the employee ceases growing in his job, while another employee may become unstable in the job. Both these cases warrant some form of counseling.

Most problems that require counseling have some emotional content. Emotions are a normal part of life. Nature gave people their emotions, and these feelings are what make people human. On the other hand, emotions can get out of control and cause workers to do things that are harmful to their own best interests as well as those of the other employees and the entire organization. They may leave their jobs because of a trifling conflict that seems large to them, or they may undermine morale in their departments. Management wants their employees to maintain good mental health and to channel their emotions along constructive lines so that all will work together effectively.

The general objective of counseling is to help employees develop better mental health so that they will grow in self-confidence, understanding, self-control and ability to work effectively. This objective is consistent with the human resources model of organizational behavior, which encourages employee growth and self-direction. It is also consistent with Maslow's higher-order needs, such as self-esteem and self-actualization. The counseling objective is achieved through one or more of the following counseling functions, which are activities performed by counseling. These are shown in *Figure 8.0.*

FIGURE 8.0 Functions of Counseling	
Advice	Telling a person what you think should be done.
Reassurance	Giving a person courage and confidence to face a problem.
Communication	Providing information and understanding.
Release of Emotional Tension	Helping a person feel freer of tensions.
Clarified Thinking	Encouraging more coherent, rational thought.
Reorientation	Encouraging an internal change in goals and values.

a. **Advice.** Many people look upon counseling as primarily an advice-giving activity, but in reality this is only one of several functions that counseling can perform. The giving of advice requires a supervisor (in a position as counselor) to make judgments about a counselee's problems and to lay out a course of action. Herein lies the difficulty, because it is almost impossible to understand another person's complicated problems, much less tell that person what to do about them. Advice-giving may breed a relationship in which the counselee feels inferior and dependent on the supervisor. In spite of all its ills, advice occurs in routine counseling because workers expect it and management tends to provide it.

b. **Reassurance.** Counseling can provide employees with reassurance, which is a way of giving them courage to face a problem or a feeling of confidence that they are pursuing a suitable course of action. One trouble with reassurance is that counselees typically do not accept it. They know that the counselor, in this case the supervisor, cannot know that the problem will come out all right. Even if they are reassured, the reassurance may fade away as soon as they face their problems again, which means that little real improvement has been made. Though reassurance has its weaknesses, it is useful in some situations and is impossible to prohibit.

c. **Communication.** Counseling can improve both upward and downward communication. In an upward direction, it is a key avenue for employees to express their feelings to management. The act of counseling initiates an upward signal, and if channels are open, some of these signals travel higher. Individual names must be kept confidential, but statements of feelings can be grouped and interpreted to management. An important part of a supervisor's job is to discover emotional problems related to company policies and to interpret those problems to top management. Counseling also achieves downward communication because supervisors help interpret and transmit company activities to employees as they discuss problems related to them.

d. **Release of Emotional Tension.** An important function of nearly all counseling is release of emotional tension. People tend to get an emotional release from their frustrations and other problems whenever they have an opportunity to tell someone about them. Although this release of tension does not necessarily solve their problems, it does remove mental blocks in the way of solutions, enabling them to face their problems again and think constructively about them. In some cases, emotional release accomplishes the whole job, dispelling an employee's problems as it they were "mental ghosts."

e. **Clarified Thinking.** Clarified thinking tends to be a normal result of emotional release, but a skilled counselor can aid this process. In order to clarify the employee's thinking, the supervisor serves as an aid only and refrains from telling the employee what is "right." Further, not all the clarified thinking takes place while the supervisor and employee are talking. All or part of it may take place later as a result of developments during the counseling relationship. The result of any clarified thinking is that a person is encouraged to accept responsibility for emotional problems and to be more realistic in solving them.

f. **Reorientation.** Another function of counseling is reorientation of the counselee. Reorientation is more than mere emotional release or clear thinking about a problem. It involves a change in the employee's psychic self through a change in the basic goals and values. For example, it can help people recognize and accept their own limitations. Reorientation is the kind of function needed to help alcoholics return to normal or to treat a person with severe mental depression. It is largely a job for professional counselors who know its uses and limitations and who have the necessary training. The supervisor's job is to recognize those in need of reorientation before their need becomes severe, so that they can be referred to professional help in time for successful treatment.

8.2   Supervisor's Counseling Role

Excluding reorientation, the other five counseling functions can be performed successfully by supervisors, assuming they have qualified themselves. They will at times perform all five of these counseling functions. On other occasions, if professional counseling services are available, they will refer employees to the professional counselors. The point is that when counseling services are established, supervisors must not conclude that all their counseling responsibilities have been transferred to the professional counselors.

Supervisors are important counselors because they are the ones having day-to-day interaction with employees. If supervisors close their eyes to the emotional problems of employees and refuse to discuss them, it would appear that they are in fact uncaring about employees' feelings and focusing their interest on the work alone. Emotions are part of the whole employee and must be considered a part of the total employment situation for which a supervisor is responsible. For this reason, all supervisors need training to help them understand problems of employees and to counsel them effectively.

Almost all problems brought to a supervisor have a combination of factual and emotional content, so a supervisor should not spend all day looking for emotional content when a rational answer will solve the problem. It is said that the father of psychiatry, Sigmund Freud, warned about the dangers of seeing emotional meaning in everything a person says or does. This is because some things simply do not have any particular emotional interpretation.

8.3 Types of Counseling

In terms of the amount of direction that a supervisor gives an employee, counseling is a continuum from full direction (*directive counseling*) to no direction (*non-directive counseling*). Between the two extremes is *participative counseling*. These three counseling types will be discussed in order to show how supervisors may vary their direction in a counseling situation.

Directive counseling is the process of listening to an employee's problem, deciding with the employee what should be done, and then telling and motivating the employee to do it. Directive counseling mostly accomplishes the counseling function of advice, but it also may reassure, communicate, give emotional release and, to a minor extent, clarify thinking. Reorientation is seldom achieved in directive counseling. Although advice is of questionable value, as usually it is not effective, some of the other functions are worthwhile. If the directive counselor is first a good listener, then the employee should feel some emotional release. As the result of emotional release plus ideas that the counselor imparts, the employee may also clarify thinking. Furthermore, useful communication probably takes place. Both advice and reassurance can be worthwhile if they give the employee more courage to take a helpful course of action that the employee supports.

Non-directive counseling is at the opposite end of the continuum. It is the process of skillfully listening and encouraging an employee to explain troublesome problems, understand them and determine appropriate solutions. It focuses on the employee rather than the counselor (supervisor) as judge and adviser, so it is "client-centered." Supervisors can use the non-directive approach but care should be taken to make sure that supervisors are not so oversold on it that they neglect their normal directive leadership responsibilities. The major difference between non-directive and directive is that in non-directive counseling, the counselee is the key person while the opposite is the case for directive counseling. In non-directive counseling, emotional release takes place even more effectively than directive counseling, and clarified thinking tends to follow. The unique advantage of non-directive counseling is its ability to cause the employee's reorientation. It emphasizes changing the person instead of dealing only with the immediate problem, in the usual manner of directive counseling. However, with all its advantages, non-directive counseling does have several limitations that restrict its use at work. First of all, it is more time-consuming and costly than directive counseling. Just one employee with one problem may require many hours of a supervisor's time, so the number of employees that a supervisor can assist is limited. Next, non-directive counseling often requires the services of professional counselors who are expensive. Non-directive counseling also depends on a capable, willing employee. It assumes that the employee possesses a drive for mental health, has enough social intelligence to perceive what problems need solution and has sufficient emotional stability to deal with them. Finally, the supervisor needs to be careful not to become a crutch for emotionally dependent employees to lean on while they avoid their work responsibilities.

Participative counseling is the type of counseling typically used in organizations. It is between the two extremes of directive and non-directive counseling, a so-called middle ground. It is a mutual supervisor-employee relationship that establishes a cooperative exchange of ideas to help solve an employee's problem. It is neither wholly counselor-centered nor counselee-centered. Rather, both mutually apply their different knowledge, perspectives and values to problems. It integrates the ideas of both participants in a counseling relationship. It is, therefore, a balanced compromise that combines many advantages of both directive and non-directive counseling while avoiding most of their disadvantages. Participative counseling starts by using the listening techniques or non-directive counseling, but as the interview progresses, supervisors play a more active role than in non-directive counseling. They offer bits of knowledge and insight and may discuss the situation from their broader knowledge of the organization, thus giving an employee a different view of the problem.

Counseling occasionally is necessary for employees because of job and personal problems that subject them to excessive stress. The conditions that tend to cause stress are called *stressors* and include work overload, time pressures, role ambiguity, financial problems and family problems. Stress affects both physical and mental health and results in burnout when it occurs chronically. The stress-performance situation indicates that excessive stress reduces job performances, but a moderate amount may help employees respond to job challenges.

9

Effective Supervisory Management

Just as in any other business, manufacturing involves a lot of hard work, frustration, new ideas, and requires the building of team spirit. Most organizations in recent years have formulated company philosophies that are oriented towards the importance of people. This is because they have come to realize that people *are* the company. It is in this field—that of focusing on people—that effective supervisory management plays an important role in helping an organization to be successful.

Although not all established organizations adopt the philosophies discussed in this chapter, it is nevertheless recognized by many management circles as being one of the most positive methods in modern management. Supervisors' number one responsibility is to help, teach and support their staff in a positive manner. This is because goals cannot simply be accomplished by pushing employees or making threats to them, but rather by providing them with the help they need to get their job done. The supervisor's job is to understand what kind of help they need and see that the staff gets it.

Supervisors, as managers, own every aspect relating to their part of the business. They divide up the various tasks and responsibilities for their group, and give ownership to individuals in their group. This is how the tasks get done. However, supervisors should not forget that they ultimately own all of it, and if one of their subordinates fails, it is the supervisor's failure for not getting them the help the subordinate needed. It is common knowledge that one person cannot do ten jobs well, but ten people can do one job well. These are the extremes, but a supervisor must find the right balance if he is to help the management be successful. As managers of their area, supervisors are responsible for finding the proper balance point, so that they use their staff efficiently and effectively while giving them a chance to do their jobs well without being overburdened. The key point is to give the right task to the right people and let them go out and be successful, as this will eventually make the organization successful.

Effective supervisors always generate team spirit. This is because they understand that if they focus on having a good, strong, enthusiastic team working for them, they will automatically be successful, as their team will ensure it. However, on a more cautious note, supervisors also need to understand that just as employees' success is their own success for having the courage to try, their failure is the supervisor's own failure for not helping them to succeed. Ultimately, the supervisor's as well as the management's success depends on the achievement of the employees.

9.1 Span of Control

Another important consideration in effective supervision is the *span of control*, which is defined as the number of employees who report directly to a supervisor.

An interesting historical contribution on span of control was provided by V.A. Graicunas, a management consultant. To Graicunas, the important consideration in establishing span of control was the number of different social relationships the supervisor is required to manage. For example, he points out that if a supervisor (A) manages two employees (B and C), there are in fact actually six different relationships, namely:

a. A with B

b. A with C

c. A with B while C is present

d. A with C while B is present

e. B to C

f. C to B

As more employees are added, the number of relationships that have to be managed multiplies. Thus, a supervisor with only twelve employees will have an almost unbelievable twenty thousand plus relationships to manage. The point that Graicunas was trying to make was that it was not enough to count only the number of bodies in a span of control, but that the numerous relationships also had to be recognized.

There is no universal formula to determine the correct span of control. The number of people who can be supervised effectively depends on variables such as the abilities and personalities of individual supervisors and subordinates, the nature of the tasks to be performed, the overall environment of the organization and the attitude of top management. In other words, only very general guidelines for effective span of control can be suggested. Each supervisor will need to consider guidelines such as the following, in light of his or her own particular personal and organizational circumstances.

Task Complexity. Generally, more complex tasks require narrower spans of control than less complex tasks.

Similarity of Tasks. If all employees within the work unit are performing similar tasks, then the span of control can be larger than when employees are performing a wide range of different activities.

Routine/Exceptional. Supervisors with workers performing routine and standard tasks, such as assembly line jobs, can usually have greater spans of control than supervisors of workers whose tasks are constantly changing, like operators who perform diagnostic failure analysis on disk drives.

Education. In organizations whose personnel are highly educated, there is a tendency to have smaller spans of control because of the complexity of jobs. However, this may be a case where larger spans could be more effective, since they would give highly educated people more autonomy.

Organizational Level. Spans of control are generally narrower at the top and broader at the bottom of the hierarchy. Like the highly educated, upper level managers may be candidates for larger spans of control.

There are some important behavioral implications inherent in wide (sometimes called "flat") spans of control and narrow (sometimes called "tall") spans. From a behavioral perspective, flat organizations are generally considered to be advantageous in that they force more responsibility onto subordinates. This results in greater employee development, more decision making at lower levels, and, consequently, greater employee satisfaction and motivation. Taller organizations have the advantage of closer control of subordinates' activities, more routes to promotion and more supervisor/employee contact. It should be added, however, that tall organizations also result in more administrative levels and activities, which may detract from getting the actual work done.

9.2 Discipline

Discipline is necessary for effective functioning of an organization. The objectives are the employees' work-related responsibilities; standards are the indexes that supervisors have established to indicate employees' progress in meeting objectives. The activities are the behaviors employees engage in to meet standards and objectives, and finally the control decision can involve discipline.

The control decision becomes positive discipline when supervisors recognize employees' progress in meeting objectives and standards and help them to develop more efficient work methods. The control decision becomes negative discipline when supervisors punish employees for deviations from standards and make no attempt to help employees correct the problem. Because discipline sometimes involves punitive control, it has a very negative connotation. This is not always justified. In fact, most employees want and respect discipline from their supervisors. This is particularly true when employees view their job as being important. Just as the members of a football team will not respect a coach who lets a star athlete drink and stay out late, employees expect their supervisors to enforce work rules and to discipline those who break them. This leads to strong pressures from the employees themselves for supervisors to use and respect discipline as a necessary part of an effective organization.

Positive discipline is said to be any control action by supervisors that results in employees' increased efficiency in attaining objectives or standards. Most often, positive discipline is associated with the "good service" approach, where the supervisor walks around smiling and encouraging people. While this kind of supervisory behavior may be appropriate, positive discipline places much greater emphasis on providing employees with feedback information or experiences that will help them attain their objectives or standards. An important part of this is rewards and recognition, but another aspect involves on-the-job training and experiences that help employees improve their effectiveness. In addition, it should be emphasized that although it may seem contradictory, positive discipline can also involve punishment, as long as that punishment facilitates the attainment of work objectives and standards. For example, a positive disciplinary approach would be to require a machine operator to clean the work area, even though it is a janitor's job if, after repeated warnings, the operator continues to leave the work area messy. In this way, the operator can experience firsthand the punishing task that would otherwise be left for others. Even though the discipline is punitive, it is very directly related to helping the operator develop a more positive attitude towards job-related objectives. Although not always advocated, it is considered to be positive discipline if handled in this way.

Negative discipline involves control by supervisors that does not aid employees in achieving their work-related objectives and standards. Both the rewarding and punishment of employee behaviors by supervisors can result in negative discipline. For example, if an employee asks a supervisor for an assessment of his or her work and the supervisor tells the employee that it was a good job when it was actually not, this is an example of negative discipline. The supervisor is rewarding the employee for poor work done and can therefore expect more poor work. Similarly, when supervisors administer punitive controls without consideration for their effect on the employees' performance, this is also a form of negative discipline. For example, supervisors who resort to disciplinary layoffs for absenteeism are usually using negative control. They are working against themselves, because the employee may get three more days of rest and relaxation in which to wonder how it can be so important to be on the job when the supervisor can lay them off for three days without worry. Discipline is only functional when it helps employees attain work-related objectives and standards.

Although there are several arguments against punitive discipline, it is nevertheless recognized that punishment is sometimes necessary. Perhaps the best approach to the use of punitive discipline is the "red-hot stove" principle. According to this approach, punishment is related to being burned by a red-hot stove. Because it is red, everyone has fair warning that the stove is extremely hot. The stove does not discriminate; it burns everyone who is foolish enough to touch it. Furthermore, the burn is automatic and immediate, and its severity depends on the degree of the person's offense.

Using the red-hot stove as a point of departure, the following guidelines are used by supervisors for the effective administration of punitive discipline in the workplace.

a. **It Should be Expected.** People need to know the rules of the game. Employees should be fully aware of the consequences of either following or not following the prescribed rules. These rules should be thoroughly communicated to employees, and they should fully expect the consequences that follow violations.

b. **There Should be a Clear Warning.** Employees should always receive a warning that they will be disciplined for inappropriate behavior. This warning should be consistent for everyone and should be issued a prescribed number of times. A warning may be sufficient to change behavior so that punishment may not be necessary.

c. **It Should be Consistent.** Supervisors should always be consistent in administering discipline.

d. **It Should be Objective.** Effective discipline does not depend on the whims and biases of the supervisor. It must be automatic and nondiscriminatory. Supervisors should set standards for behavior and performance. Although it is difficult not to be biased, as supervisors are not always available to observe employee behavior, employees will still respect the supervisor if he makes a conscientious effort to avoid bias.

e. **It Should be Immediate.** Effective discipline closely follows the infraction. This immediate reaction helps clarify the reasons for the discipline because the employee still vividly remembers the behavior.

f. **It Should be Impersonal.** Effective discipline does not become a personal attack on employees. Discipline should be administered so that employees know that it is their behavior with which their supervisors find fault, not themselves.

g. It Should be Fair. Finally, employees must feel that they have been treated fairly, that "the punishment fits the crime." That is, the intensity of the discipline should closely match the infraction that has occurred.

Effective discipline is an important function of supervision. Supervisors must have the ability to understand and effectively use positive and negative approaches to discipline in the workplace.

9.3 Controlling for Results

Controls are an integral and unavoidable part of life for all modern organizations. Within organizations, a variety of controls are used, such as budgets, schedules, audits and inventory reports, to mention only a few.

Controls may be defined as a process, active or passive, for regulating organizational activities to ensure that they contribute to effective performance. Inherent within this control process are four important elements: objectives, standards, activities and decisions. Briefly, the process begins with a set of objectives for the effective performance of the organization. In most organizations, these objectives are incorporated into the planning activities during the initial phase of the processes; examples include network plans and management by objectives (MBO). If the objectives of these plans are to be viable, however, they have to be further scaled down and translated into standards of performance. That is, there must be a specific yardstick that indicates when the plan has been achieved and, preferably, indicates progress or benchmarks towards achieving the plan. This standard is the activity that can be measured. The activity measurement is then compared with the standard to indicate progress. Up to this point, the control process is very closely related to the planning process. The last step of the control process is the control decision. Generally, if the activity measurements meet the desired standards, the supervisor would make a passive decision not to act. However, when activities do not measure up to standards, then an active decision is necessary.

A control decision can take three general forms. First, the supervisor may decide that the objectives of the plan are unrealistic; therefore, they would have to be either modified or eliminated. Second, it may be decided that the standards are inappropriate. That is, the basic objectives and guidelines in the plan may remain intact, but it may be decided that the specific standards relating to volume of work, time allotted or resources expended must be made more realistic. Finally, the supervisor may make a decision to change the quality or quantity of activity necessary to achieve the plan. An extra employee may be added or subtracted, additional equipment may be borrowed or purchased or there may be a change in the supply of materials.

Feed-Forward Control. This category is a relatively new concept. The rationale behind feed-forward control is that the damage has already been done if the first control decision is made after the objectives, standards and activities have all been completed. For example, it does little good when a supervisor who burns out a $150,000 machine and loses $60,000 in production waiting for a replacement, plans, for a preventive maintenance program. Thus, according to the feed-forward concept of control, supervisors must work through the process beforehand and make control decisions before crises occur. Some examples of feed-forward control mechanisms include: policies that become predetermined courses of action for a given set of conditions, warning signs or signals, checklists and prescreening on the quality of inputs to the process. The whole purpose of these mechanisms and the perspective of feed-forward control in general is to anticipate and prevent.

As stated earlier, the control process (at least the first three steps) is very closely related to the planning process. The major difference between them is that plans are futuristic and concern an organization's intentions. Controls, on the other hand, are an active and immediate process. They incorporate all the elements of planning but add the additional ingredient of active decisions to change organizational objectives, standards or activities to ensure that the organization is performing according to the plans that have been set out.

The two main categories of control mechanisms that are usually considered in an organization are in-process control and feed-back control.

In-Process Control. In this category of control, the idea is that it may be possible to apply controls in a more efficient manner at the process stage rather than waiting for the outcome. A good example of in-process control is the gasoline gauge on a car that shows a continuous measure that lets the driver know beforehand when gas is needed. Examples of in-process control systems in today's organization include: real-time computer systems that provide essential reports such as inventory, numerical counters that record the number of completed units automatically and automatic switches that shut off a system in a state of emergency. In-process controls represent the middle ground. They do not necessarily anticipate problems as in feed-forward, but instead monitor performance while it is happening.

Feed-back Control. The second category is the after-the-fact feed-back control. We need to distinguish this from the other uses of "feed-back," hence, the use of the hyphen on this term. This feed-back occurs when the process is complete. Of course, feed-back is the most common, but perhaps the least desirable form of control since it occurs after the problem has taken place. It is directed towards correctly detecting future deviations in performance. Examples of methods of obtaining feed-back for control include the following: accounting reports, performance appraisals, quality control on finished goods and monthly reports. In recent times, however, the emphasis on feed-back control is changing and the movement is towards converting it into feed-forward or in-process controls. This conversion process can be illustrated by using one of the same examples stated earlier—performance appraisals. Here feed-forward control can be exercised by setting objectives with employees and providing daily or weekly coaching and assessment rather than waiting until the end of the year.

10

Concluding Thoughts

This final chapter attempts to look into some of the major changes that should affect supervision in the future. If the rate of change of the coming years is anywhere close to that experienced in the past, many radical changes will be forthcoming. It is hoped that some of the projections and possible strategies offered in this study will enable supervisors to be better prepared for forthcoming changes and to find ways of adapting to change and progress while at the same time improving their work.

10.1 The Changing Environment

There is certainly no doubt that in the future, supervisors will be facing a different environment than the one they are facing today or have faced in the past. Knowledge of the expectant future and the ability and the willingness to adapt to, as well as to manage, this change can make the difference between effective and ineffective performance.

The advance of technology can be thought of in terms of a speeding car where the surrounding landscape becomes more and more obscure and finally ends in a blur. Each technological discovery opens the way for many more new discoveries. As a result, the environment facing supervisors in the future will reflect even greater technological sophistication. In many organizations, supervisors will be unable to understand all aspects of their employees' jobs. As a result, two trends in supervision, which have already appeared, should become more pronounced in the future. First, participative supervisory styles will become more relevant and necessary. Only through cooperative, participative styles will supervisors be able to obtain the information necessary to make their decisions. Second, supervisors are going to have to place more trust in their employees and give them more autonomy. In many cases, the supervisor will simply not have the facts or expertise to make important job-related decisions. As a result, they will have to delegate more decision-making responsibilities to employees and will have to place confidence and trust in them. As technological sophistication increases and the resulting gap between supervisors' authority and their knowledge of subordinates' jobs widens, more participation and trust will become necessary.

Computers are being widely used in all organizational activities. Thus, supervisors in many different kinds of organizations have already experienced or can expect to see some definite changes in their jobs because of the computer.

The most important changes brought about by the computer can be summarized as follows:

a. **Information-Gathering and Record Keeping.** Supervisors have traditionally been the focal point for collecting and assembling information. In the future, supervisors will increasingly be asked to supply the input data for computerized information systems. Where possible, supervisors should delegate data-gathering activities so that they will not become merely glorified file clerks.

b. **Problem-Solving.** Both the speed and accuracy of the computer can be of very decided help to supervisors in solving problems. Calculations that used to take weeks to work out can now be done in a matter of minutes. Importantly, however, the computer's major function should always be viewed as that of providing data and information. The decision itself should always be made by the person interpreting the information.

c. **Communication Link.** As computers are used more and more frequently to store, retrieve and process information, supervisory positions will be viewed by many as the focal point for distributing this information. In many ways, this is not a great change from traditional communication patterns. However, the computer will provide supervisors with much more information and they will have to become much more skilled in analyzing and interpreting it.

d. **Centralized Control.** Because the computer is capable of processing information rapidly, it is becoming much easier for top management to keep close tabs on lower-level operations. Already it is possible in some organizations for top management to determine the exact, instantaneous output of a particular unit by merely punching a few keys on a terminal. Access to this type of information will become much more common in the future and will undoubtedly make for more top management control decisions that were formerly handled by supervisors.

e. **Loss of Power.** Another danger that may result from the impact of computers is the loss of power by many supervisors. For example, the computer would enable all personnel records to be centralized, thus becoming the responsibility of the personnel department. The personnel manager could then be given the authority to deal with all disciplinary matters, such as absenteeism. Although this approach would have the advantage of ensuring that all discipline would be uniform and non-discriminatory, it would also seriously erode the power of the front line supervisor who traditionally handles these matters. Supervisory authority has already been eroded in many functions, such as wage and salary administration. Thus, in the future, supervisors may find that even more of their important responsibilities are being stripped away. Additionally, government regulation, changing nature of the work force and increased accountability will also affect supervisors in the coming years. The government is becoming increasingly involved in all aspects of organizational activity, and this trend will undoubtedly hold for the future. Areas already greatly affected by government regulations include:

a. safety

b. emissions and waste disposal

c. product liability

d. labor relations

e. employment practices

A few decades ago, there was such a thing as the "stereotype" working person. Today, if anything, there is no typical worker. Workers may be male or female, come from different races and religions and speak different languages. They could also be handicapped, be under twenty-one or over sixty-five years of age. To an extent, of course, the increased participation of these minority groups in the work force is a function of government legislation. Yet it must be remembered that the laws really reflect the changes in our society. News stories of medical and legal malpractice suits have one thing in common—that is, people were eventually blamed and held accountable for their actions. This indicates the fact that, today, people will continue to demand responsible action from public officials and hold them directly accountable when their actions are not appropriate. Correspondingly, supervisors can be viewed the same way by their people. Employees are beginning to demand that supervisors be held accountable for their actions.

10.2 Increased Professionalization of Supervisors

Other likely developments in the future include more closely-knit professional organizations and a professional orientation for supervisors. This trend probably stems from the increasing pride in being a supervisor, increasing educational requirements for being a supervisor and the growing split with top management on the one side and the rank-and-file employees on the other.

The first factor, pride resulting in professionalism, comes from the growing recognition that supervisory positions are very demanding and require special knowledge and abilities. As supervisors become more and more aware of this, they begin to see themselves as professionals. This ties in very well with job satisfaction. A second factor resulting in increased professionalization is the higher level of education for supervisors and its standardization. With the level of education increasing for everyone, some supervisory jobs are currently requiring a degree qualification and more employers will no doubt be making such demands in the future. It is also becoming increasingly apparent that there is a common body of knowledge that supervisors should have assimilated and be able to apply. The subject matter of this study, to a certain extent, represents this body of supervisory knowledge and contributes to the professionalization of supervisors.

Increased pressures from both the top and bottom levels of organizations are literally forcing supervisors to unify and identify themselves as a distinct professional group. In several large organizations, for example, wages paid to unionized hourly workers have equaled and even surpassed the salaries of their supervisors. In reaction to this, supervisors can unionize themselves, and in a few cases they have done so. The other approach is to adopt a more professional viewpoint and to demand the rewards that go with professionalism. In the long run, the latter route would seem to be in the best interest of individual supervisors, their organizations and society. Supervisors must become professionals in terms of outlook, but this, of course, does not or should not prevent them from unionizing. Many factors indicate that supervisors in the future will have a much more challenging and complex job than they have had in the past. If supervisors are able to respond to these challenges, they should be able to retain a position of importance in the organizations of the future.

10.3 Strategy for Supervisory Success

We have observed that the work of the supervisor is difficult and complex. Supervisory effectiveness requires people who are technically competent, bright and possess good people management skills. Such supervisors are aware of what goes on around them. They realize that we live in a changing world and that we must be ready to adjust to the new conditions. These conditions have added new dimensions to the supervisor's responsibilities. Now they also have to be economic advocates as well as effective communicators. They must choose to facilitate more often. When the challenges of the job are met, the personal satisfactions are substantial. The organization meets its goal through the important contributions of supervisors.

Noted below are some key points for personal success for supervisors. Also listed are cautions for supervisors to take note of.

A STRATEGY FOR SUCCESS

a. **Make a Commitment.** Although achieving supervisory success is a challenge, it can be done. The first step is to decide if supervisors really want to make the effort to be exceptional. The thing to take note of here is that emphasis is on "effort" and "exceptional." Supervisors "get by" all the time. But to be effective demands working at developing supervisory skills, and any time real effort is involved, commitment is required.

b. The Ten Percent Factor. What is not usually understood is that the difference between "getting by" and being exceptional is relatively small. It is probably on the order of ten percent. Being only ten percent better than the average person is enough to separate one supervisor from the pack.

c. Sustaining the Effort. It is not enough to be effective part of the time—it must be sustained. Supervisors must realize that the skills and gains that they are making are cumulative. The ten percent gained serves as a new base level of measurement.

d. People. Supervisors cannot do it all, so the need is there to go after good employees. Supervisory excellence will serve as a magnet to draw good employees. Talented staff are sometimes hard to supervise. It must be noted, however, that although they demand a lot, they give a lot in return. Supervisors must select their staff wisely and see that they are trained and developed. Supervisors must know their people as individuals as well as members of the work group and lead them accordingly. Although supervisors have a limited budget for granting pay raises and promotions are not always possible, they have an unlimited "budget" for passing out praises to deserving employees and they must use it.

e. Be Skillful. Supervisors must stay on top of technological, procedural and other changing job conditions. Reading professional journals on supervisory management topics may be useful. Additionally, supervisors may join professional management institutes to keep abreast of the latest developments.

f. Looking after Assets. Supervisors must maintain and protect all the equipment, tools, materials and information entrusted to them.

g. Plan and Act. Skillful planning is what puts one supervisor on top of the rest. Learning how to plan is vital. Anticipating and identifying potential problems that can be a stumbling block, in order to solve them, is also important.

h. **Paying Attention to the Little Things.** Supervisors who know all the details of their jobs will find that they have few unpleasant surprises. Almost every big problem that supervisors face today began as a little problem sometime in the past.

SOME POINTS OF CAUTION

a. **Failure to Ask for Help.** We all need help at one time or another—supervisors are no exception. Supervisors should seek assistance if they require it and not mislead themselves into believing that they can work out every problem by themselves.

b. **Failure to Communicate.** Supervisors must not assume that people always know what is happening. They must exercise good judgment and pass on relevant information upward, downward and laterally to their colleagues.

c. **Failure to Acknowledge.** It is important for supervisors to highlight their employees' accomplishments, as this shows that the supervisor is proud of the team and its achievements.

d. **Failure to Press.** Employees must always be pushed to do their best. However, supervisors must be sensitive to excessive pressure on people. Although stress is a way to reach full potential, too much stress can lead to breakdown in performance and personal confidence.

e. **Failure to Understand Things before Change Takes Place.** Effective supervisors are people of action. But they act wisely. They make sure that they fully appreciate the reasons for things being the way they are. Once this is understood, then, if change is necessary, steps should be taken to introduce them.

f. **Failure to Use What is Available.** More or newer is not always better. Nor is it necessarily economically possible for an organization. Supervisors should always reconsider what they have before asking for more.

In the final analysis, however, it is still the thinking, hard-working individual who gets ahead. As in every other life situation, a person gets out of a career whatever he or she puts in. It is hoped that by understanding and using the concepts and skills presented in this study, the supervisor can become more effective in the job.

Index

A

Advertising for Recruitment 53
Administrative Duties 21

B

Budget Forecast 36

C

Centralized Control 121
Changing Environment 119
Channels of Communication 71
Communication and People 70
Controlling for Results 114
Controls 18
Counseling, Functions of 98

D

Directive Counseling 102
Direct Orders 75
Direct Supervision, Effects of 86
Discipline 110

F

Feedback 90
Feedback Control 116
Feed-Forward Control 115

G

Goal-Setting and Path Improvement 89

I

Industrial Relations 14
Induction (Orientation) Programs 60
In-Process Control 116
Internal/External Recruitment 51
Interviews and Handling Grievances 76

J

Job Specification 49

L

Learning Curve 66
Levels of Management 10
Link Person 8
Loss of Power 121

M

Major Areas of Supervisory
  Responsibilities 17
Manager 9
Manpower Needs 44
Meetings 78
Morale, Job Satisfaction & Productivity 84
Motion Study 42

N

Non-Directive Counseling 103

O

Objectives of Performance Appraisals 92
Office Equipment 22
Off-the-Job Training (Off-JT) 68
On-the-Job Training (OJT) 66

P

Participative Counseling 104
Performance Appraisals 91
Planning Process 33
Production Planning & Control 39
Production Capacity 42
Professionalization of Supervisors 123
Project Checklist 26
Project Reports 24
Project Timetable 26

R

Recruitment   47
Recruitment & Selection Process   48

S

Safety   27
Safety in the Workplace   30
Selection   55
Span of Control   108
Staff Problems   12
Strategy for Supervisory Success   124
Supervision and the Organization   8
Supervisors as Communicators   74
Supervisor as Discussion Leader   80
Supervisor's Counseling Role   101
Supervisor's Role in Training   62

T

Technical Competence of Supervisor   16
Total Quality Management (TQM)   41
Training & Development   59

U

Unions and Staff Associations   73

W

Work Environment   87
Work Measurement   42
Work Roles of Subordinates   11

MELLEN STUDIES IN BUSINESS

1. Khalid R. Mehtabdin, **Comparative Management: Business Styles in Japan and the United States**

2. Donald G. Jones and Patricia Bennett (eds.), **A Bibliography of Business Ethics, 1981-1985**

3. Giichi Sugimoto, **Six-Sided Management: Righteousness, Gratitude, Compassion**

4. Alexander J. Matejko. **A Christian Approach To Work and Industry**

5. Daniel Metraux, **The Japanese Economy and the American Businessman**

6. Mohammed Salleh and Donald Grunewald, **Supervisory Management and Its Link to the Human Resources Function**

7. Karen Paul, **Contemporary Issues in Business Ethics and Politics**

8. Karen Paul, **Contemporary Issues in Business and Society in the United States and Abroad**

9. Jacqueline Tak-York Cheung and Kwong-Leung Tang, **Models of Workplace Training: Lessons From the Employees Retraining Scheme in Hong Kong**

10. Donald Grunewald and Sol Shaviro, **The Complete Book of Management**

11. Samuel Schneider, **Three American Economics Professors Battle Against Monopoly and Pricing Practices: Ripley, Fetter and Commons: "Three for the People"**

12. Jess S. Boronico (ed.), **Studies in the Strategy and Tactics of Competitive Advantage: Management in the New Millennium**

13. Kevin W. Sightler, **A Bibliographic Resource on Entrepreneurship, Self-Defeating Behaviors, and the Fears of Success and Failure**

14. Rick D. Saucier, **Influencing Sales Through Store Design**

15. Ivan M. Manev, **The Managerial Network in a Multinational Enterprise**

16. Fred W. Becker, **Problems in Privatization Theory and Practice in State and Local Governments**

17. James W. Westerman, **The Impact of Person-Organization Fit on Employee Attitudes and Outcomes**